DON'T BE PISSED WHEN YOU LEARN THE BENEFITS OF URINE THERAPY

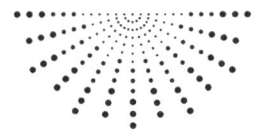

SKYE ANGELOU

SKYE ANGELOU PUBLISHING

INTRODUCTION TO URINE THERAPY

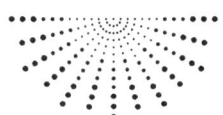

*U*rine therapy, alternatively known as urotherapy or auto-urine therapy, is a unique and time-honored practice where individuals harness the potential therapeutic benefits of their own urine. While unconventional, this practice has been woven into the fabric of various cultures across centuries, offering a fascinating perspective on holistic well-being.

Embracing the Positives

Contrary to initial skepticism, urine therapy has emerged as a subject of interest due to its reported positive impact on health. Numerous cultures have embraced this practice, attributing it to a range of natural remedies for internal and external ailments, such as skin conditions, digestive issues, and infections. The belief in urine's ability to house antibodies, enzymes, and hormones that can fortify the immune system adds a layer of intrigue to its potential health benefits.

Unveiling the Immune-Boosting Potential

One of the noteworthy aspects of urine therapy is its purported ability to enhance the immune system. Despite its origins as a bodily waste product, urine contains various substances that stimulate the production of antibodies and white blood cells. This stimulation contributes to the body's defense against infections, complemented by potential anti-inflammatory properties found in urine therapy.

Exploring Unconventional Health Perspectives

The historical backdrop of urine therapy includes significant figures such as Mahatma Gandhi, who endorsed its use for diverse health concerns. Even in contemporary times, notable personalities, including Bear Grylls and Lady Gaga, have openly embraced this unconventional practice, adding a modern twist to an ancient tradition.

Beyond the Skepticism

Moving beyond skepticism, some enthusiasts explore the potential benefits of urine therapy for skin and hair health, believing it may even possess anti-aging effects. Cosmetic applications, including the treatment of skin diseases like eczema and insect bites, continue to find a place for urine therapy in various cultural practices.

Navigating Limited Research

While scientific research on urine therapy remains limited, certain studies suggest that urine contains compounds with antimicrobial and anti-inflammatory effects.

Balancing Caution and Curiosity

Caution is fundamental when considering urine therapy, as improper storage or consumption may expose individuals to health risks. It is imperative to emphasize that urine therapy should only be undertaken under the guidance of healthcare professionals, acknowledging its potential side effects and limitations.

In Conclusion

In conclusion, urine therapy, though unconventional, has been explored for its potential health benefits, spanning immune system enhancement, potential anti-cancer properties, and contributions to skin health. As the conversation around alternative health practices continues, an open-minded exploration of urine therapy may provide insights into its potential positive effects. However, due diligence, professional guidance, and an individualized approach are essential before embarking on such a unique wellness journey.

THE HISTORY BEHIND URINE THERAPY

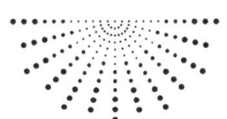

Urine therapy, also known as urotherapy or auto-urine therapy, is a practice in which an individual consumes or applies their own urine for therapeutic purposes. Although this practice may seem unorthodox, it has been used in various cultures for centuries and has been studied for its potential health benefits.

There are several reported benefits of urine therapy, including its use as a natural remedy for a variety of ailments, both internal and external, including skin conditions, digestive problems, and infections. Urine is believed to contain antibodies, enzymes, and hormones that can help boost the body's immune system and fight off illness.

Still a skeptic! Do not rule it out just yet.

One of the potential benefits of urine therapy is its ability to boost the immune system.

How is this possible, being a waste product from the body? Keep reading!

Urine contains a variety of substances that can stimulate the production of antibodies and white blood cells, which can help the body fight off infections and diseases. Additionally, urine therapy may also have anti-inflammatory properties, which can further support the immune system.

Urine therapy has also been studied for its potential anti-cancer properties. A study published in the Journal of Cancer Research and Therapeutics found that urine therapy was effective in inhibiting the growth of cancer cells in vitro. The researchers suggest that this may be due to the presence of compounds in urine that have anti-tumor properties.

One of the most renowned proponents of urine therapy was Indian nationalist leader Mahatma Gandhi, who reportedly drank his urine as a form of medicine. In his autobiography, Gandhi wrote that he used urine therapy to treat everything from constipation to snakebite. Decades later, Prime Minister Modi tried convincing the US of the significance of urine therapy.

Did it work? You can be the judge of that.

Today, lots of people, including celebrities, drink their own urine for various reasons, like TV survival expert Bear Grylls, Lady Gaga, and others.

Moving on to other potentials of urine therapy!

Some people believe that urine can help improve the appearance of the skin and hair and may even have anti-aging effects. Hence, it is utilized for cosmetic purposes, including curing skin diseases like eczema, rashes, and uneven skin tones. It is also a cure for insect and reptile bites and is used in many areas, even in Africa.

While there is limited scientific research on the benefits of urine therapy, some studies have suggested that urine contains compounds that may have antimicrobial and anti-inflammatory effects, as many people continue to indulge in urine therapy as a natural remedy for many diseases.

However, it is essential to note that urine can also contain harmful substances, such as bacteria and toxins, especially if the person is taking medication or has an underlying medical condition. It is important to note that urine therapy should only be practiced under the guidance of a healthcare professional, as it may not be appropriate for everyone and may have potential side effects.

In conclusion, while urine therapy may seem unconventional, it has been studied for its potential health benefits, including boosting the immune system, inhibiting the growth of cancer cells, and improving skin health. However, more research is needed to fully understand the benefits and risks of this practice and make it more acceptable to a wider audience.

DEFINITION OF URINE THERAPY

If you are reading this book, you have probably heard of the incredible benefits of drinking one's urine, but you want to know more. It is understandable, and if you are skeptical about the process, this section will define urine therapy and all its aliases.

Before we jump into the definition, urine therapy is a form of alternative medicine with centuries of positive results that is still in practice in many regions of the world and dates back to ancient Rome, Greece, China, and India.

So what is urine therapy?

This is a practice that involves consuming one's own urine or applying it topically to the skin or other body parts. Advocates of urine therapy believe that urine contains various beneficial substances, such as urea, uric acid, and other minerals, that can help improve health and treat diverse medical conditions. This claim will be discussed in chapter two, so keep reading.

Moving on!

Urine therapy has various names and aliases, some of which include Orin therapy, urotherapy, urophagia, urinotherapy, and more. Some of these are discussed below:

1. Uropathy: This is a more general term used to describe the act of using urine for medicinal purposes. It encompasses all forms of urine therapy, including internal and external uses like drinking or applying on the skin.

2. Amaroli: This is a term used in Ayurvedic medicine and an ancient therapeutic and spiritual healing technique employed by yogis. This practice involves consuming your own urine or massaging it into the body to optimize one's overall health. Believers also claim that urine therapy can help to balance the three doshas (vata, pitta, and kapha) and promote overall health and well-being.

3. Shivambu: This is another term used in Ayurvedic medicine to describe the practice of urine therapy. This technique is based on an old belief that classifies urine as a 'holy liquid' used to keep the

body healthy. Shivambu is a two-word derived from the Sanskrit words "Shiva" (meaning auspicious) and "Ambu" (meaning water) and is believed to have spiritual and healing properties.

4. Auto-urine therapy: This term is often used to describe the practice of consuming one's urine. It is sometimes referred to as auto-urotherapy or auto-urine injection therapy.

5. Urine fasting: This practice involves consuming only your urine and water for some time, usually several days to a week or more. Proponents of urine fasting believe it can help to detoxify the body and improve overall health.

Despite its long history and various names and aliases, urine therapy remains a controversial practice in modern medicine. While users of this therapy claim that it can be used to treat a wide range of medical conditions, including cancer, diabetes, and autoimmune disorders, there is little scientific evidence to support these claims.

Most doctors are against this therapy, claiming it is dangerous and unhealthy for the human body.

Keep in mind they are trained only in medicine and surgery so they will not be able to best advise you.

My Thoughts

My question, however, is: if there is no valid evidence against it, why disregard the reports from people who have tried it with successful results?

Humans are afraid of trying new things. Drinking your urine does not sound or feel appealing, but rather than rule out an option for maintaining good health, do more research for yourself. This book is a prompt to awaken you to the many alternatives to healthy living within your reach.

HISTORY AND CULTURAL SIGNIFICANCE OF URINE THERAPY

Drinking urine has fascinated people for centuries; it has attracted people and been given all wonderful names, like the "elixir of long life", "liquid gold', "gold of blood," or the rejuvenation liquid in Shivambu. Whether you believe in the therapeutic potentials of "waste" products having a healing property depends on you.

However, drinking urine is registered in Hindu texts dating back to 5000 years and is used as therapy for arthritis, acne, allergies, migraines, and skin diseases. This practice moved from India to other regions in the world, including the Aztec Empire, Egypt, China, Rome, and today, everywhere.

Some say urine therapy or urine consumption originated from the Indian culture, but others claim it goes way back. Regardless of where it started, it is changing an aspect of alternative medicine and defiling the reputation of orthodox medicine.

As mentioned, the earliest known record of urine therapy comes from ancient India, where it was known as Amaroli or Shivambu Kalpa. In Ayurveda, a traditional Indian system of medicine, urine therapy is considered a form of urotherapy and is used to treat a range of ailments, from skin diseases to digestive issues, and respiratory problems.

Urine therapy in the Renaissance period

While the practice of urine therapy has been used in various cultures throughout history, it gained popularity in Europe during the Renaissance period (14th–17th centuries).

Urine therapy was commonly used by doctors as a diagnostic tool during the Renaissance. They would examine the color, smell, and taste of a patient's urine to determine their overall health and diagnose various diseases. In addition to diagnosis, urine was also used in treating a diverse range of illnesses, including fever, headache, and even the Black Plague.

During the Renaissance period, one of the most famous proponents of urine therapy was Swiss physician Paracelsus. Paracelsus believed that urine contained essential substances that could be used to treat a variety of ailments, and he prescribed it for everything from skin conditions to epilepsy. History also recorded that he collected from people who ate cabbage (do not know why) to cure skin cancer.

In addition to its medical uses, urine was also used for cosmetic purposes during the Renaissance period. It was believed that urine could be used to whiten teeth, cure gum diseases, soften and clear the skin, and even cure baldness.

While urine therapy was widely accepted during the Renaissance period, it eventually fell out of favor as medical knowledge advanced and more effective treatments were discovered. Today, the practice is still used by some alternative medicine practitioners, but it is not widely accepted by the medical community.

Urine Therapy in China

The practice of urine therapy also has roots in Chinese medicine. In the Huangdi Neijing, a Chinese medical text dating back to around 200 BCE, urine is described as having therapeutic properties and is recommended as a treatment for various conditions. In traditional Chinese medicine, urine therapy is known to treat a wide range of ailments, including arthritis, cancer, and diabetes. In addition, some Chinese medicine practitioners believe that drinking one's own urine can help prevent and treat certain types of infections.

Urine therapy also has cultural significance in other parts of the world. In many African cultures, urine is believed to have powerful healing properties and is used to treat many ailments, including snakebites, wounds, and fever.

Similarly, in some Native American cultures, urine is considered a sacred substance and is used in various healing ceremonies. For example, in the Navajo tradition, urine is used as a purification substance, and it is believed to have the power to cleanse both the body and the mind.

Urine therapy in modern times

In the Western world, urine therapy is generally considered a controversial and unproven practice with minimal scientific evidence. While many still kick against consuming urine as a waste product of the body, we live in the 21st century, and the Western world is mesmerized by the ideology of the East. The lifestyle, health style, eating habits, and practice are incorporated in the West.

For example, by eating fermented foods and raw fish and practicing mindfulness, yoga, and meditation, these ancient Oriental cultures crept upon us, and we found them unburdened.

So why is urine therapy such a terrible thing?

After all, we have incorporated other healing therapies like acupuncture, chakra, and yoga for relieving stress, mental issues, or physical injury. Urine therapy, on the other hand, is a little hard to swallow, whether mentally or physically.

However, today, urine therapy has gained popularity in the West, particularly among proponents of alternative medicine. Advocates of urine therapy claim that it can help treat a range of conditions, including acne, allergies, cancer, and even HIV/AIDS.

While there is little scientific evidence to support these claims, some studies have suggested that urine may contain beneficial compounds, such as urea and creatinine, which could have therapeutic effects. For example, a study published in the Journal of Ethnopharmacology found that urine from healthy individuals contains a range of bioactive compounds that could have antimicrobial and anti-inflammatory properties.

Despite the potential benefits of urine therapy, there are also risks associated with consuming or applying urine. Urine can contain harmful substances, such as bacteria, viruses, and toxins, which can cause illness or infection. In addition, urine therapy can be psychologically distressing for some individuals and can lead to social stigma and isolation.

In conclusion, urine therapy has a long and diverse history, with cultural significance in many parts of the world. While the practice has gained popularity in the West as a form of alternative medicine, there is little scientific evidence to support its use. While urine may contain beneficial compounds, there are also risks associated with consuming or applying it, and individuals should exercise caution and seek medical advice before using urine as a form of therapy.

MISCONCEPTIONS AND COMMON CRITICISMS OF URINE THERAPY

Despite its long history of use in traditional medicine and anecdotal reports of its benefits, urine therapy is often met with skepticism and criticism. Some common misconceptions and criticisms of urine therapy include:

1. Urine therapy can cure all sickness: this is a common misconception and it is not true. There are amazing cure by urine

therapy but it is definitely not a cure for all sickness.

2. Urine is dirty and full of toxins. While urine does contain waste products and toxins, it is mostly composed of water and other harmless substances such as urea, creatinine, and electrolytes. The idea that urine is dirty or toxic is a myth and has been debunked by scientific research.

3. Urine is sterile: if you agree with this then where are the healing properties that endears to users. It is not true as urine contains a host of bacteria some good and some not so good. When urine leaves the body it is termed sterile and if stored well, it will remain so or be a breeding ground for harmful pathogens that can be infectious to the body

4. Urine therapy is unhygienic: While the idea of drinking or applying urine may seem unhygienic or unsanitary to some people, urine is actually a sterile substance when it leaves the body. As long as the urine is collected and stored properly, there is little risk of contamination or infection.

5. Urine therapy is a pseudoscientific practice. While there is limited scientific research on urine therapy, there is some evidence to suggest that it may have potential health benefits. For example, urine contains small amounts of vitamins, hormones, and other beneficial substances that may have therapeutic effects.

6. Urine therapy is not backed by mainstream medicine. While urine therapy is not widely accepted or practiced by mainstream medicine, there are some alternative health practitioners who believe in its potential benefits. However, it is important to note that alternative therapies should never be used as a substitute for conventional medical treatment.

7. Urine therapy is a dangerous practice. While there are some risks associated with urine therapy, such as the potential for infection or allergic reactions, these risks are relatively low if the urine is collected and used properly. However, individuals with certain medical conditions, such as kidney disease or

diabetes, should avoid urine therapy altogether.

8. Urine therapy can cure fungi infection: many people say urine is a great way to treat athlete's foot but medical people say, one would need more urea percentage that what is found in urine to eliminate a fungi infection.
9. Urine therapy is a cure for cancer: Urine contains some tumor inducing protein that is believed to inhibit cancer growth. Hence users believe consuming it can trigger the body to produce anti-bodies that will fight protein cancer cells
10. Urine can help remove excess mucus from bronchial tubes by inhaling it is a huge myth and while some say it works, it is a stretch that this process actually clears the lungs or bronchial tubes.

Overall, while urine therapy may not be for everyone and its benefits are still a topic of debate, it is important to approach it with an open mind and to consider all of the available evidence before making a decision about its use.

CONCLUSION

Urine therapy, the practice of using one's own urine for health and wellness purposes, has been a part of traditional medicine in many cultures for centuries. Although it may seem unappealing to some, there is evidence from real-life users to suggest that it can have some health benefits.

Urine contains various compounds and nutrients that can have therapeutic effects, such as urea, creatinine, and hormones. These compounds can help improve digestion, boost the immune system, and even act as an anti-inflammatory agent. More on the urine component in the next chapter!

While there is limited scientific research on the efficacy of urine therapy, many individuals have reported positive results after trying it, including improved skin health, increased energy, and reduced symptoms of various health conditions.

It is important to note that urine therapy is not for the faint-hearted and, it is a thing of the mind. You have to be mentally prepared to indulge in urine therapy. However, alternative medicine is not only appealing but worth all the hype. Furthermore, for those who are curious about alternative approaches to health and wellness, urine therapy may be worth a trial.

As with any new health practice, it is important to speak with a healthcare professional, urine therapy experts, or people who have successfully applied and ingested urine before diving in. Lastly, ensure it is safe and appropriate for you before you start.

3

THE SCIENCE BEHIND
URINE THERAPY

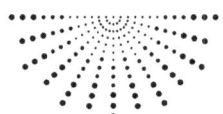

*H*umans' curiosity and fascination with urine dates back millennia. In reality, it was always seen as a distilled product selected from the blood that included useful components for the maintenance of the body, rather than as a waste product of the body. A number of names were given to it, such as "gold of the blood" and "elixir of long life," which both allude to its curative properties.

Many ailments, including viral or bacterial infections, have been linked to the consumption of freshly voided morning urine. Nausea, vomiting, headache, palpitations, diarrhea, and fever are all common complaints among those who try drinking urine for the first time. Urine contains a variety of chemicals that may play a significant role in the body, including urea, uric acid, cytokines, hormones, and urokinase. Embrocations, compresses for local tumors, a full body or foot bath in urine, eye drops, ear drops, or nose drops made from urine, and wound cleansing with urine are all examples of local urine therapies.

THIS CHAPTER PROVIDES a scientific explanation for urine therapy, which has its roots in Indian culture, and a brief history of the practice across time and geography. Urine therapy has been used for centuries, with evidence dating back to the Egyptians, Jews, Greeks, Romans, Middle Ages, and Renaissance. It has also been used more recently, from the 18th century to the current day.

URINE THERAPY, a practice deeply rooted in Indian culture, has fascinated and perplexed societies across time and geography. Despite its unconventional nature, it has stood the test of centuries, leaving a historical trail that stretches from ancient civilizations to contemporary times. In this chapter, we delve into the scientific aspects of urine therapy, exploring its historical roots and its enduring presence in diverse cultures.

Scientific Explanation of Urine Therapy

Composition of Urine

To comprehend the potential scientific basis of urine therapy, one must first examine the composition of urine. Urine is primarily composed of water, electrolytes, urea, creatinine, and various trace elements. Urea, in particular, is a nitrogenous waste product that plays a crucial role in the excretion of excess nitrogen from the body.

Antibacterial Properties

Studies have indicated that urine possesses antibacterial properties, primarily due to substances like urea. Urea, when applied topically or consumed, can create an environment unfavorable for the growth of certain bacteria. This antibacterial aspect aligns with historical uses of urine therapy for wound healing and combating infections.

Immunological Factors

Urine also contains components of the immune system, including antibodies and white blood cells. These elements contribute to the body's defense mechanisms, fostering the idea that urine therapy could potentially stimulate the immune system. The presence of lymphocytes and macrophages in urine suggests an immunological aspect that aligns with traditional beliefs in its healing properties.

Hormonal Content

Another facet of urine therapy lies in its hormonal content. Hormones such as melatonin, serotonin, and cortisol have been detected in urine. Advocates of urine therapy propose that the ingestion or topical application of urine may contribute to hormonal balance and overall well-being.

Anti-Inflammatory Potential

Research has hinted at the anti-inflammatory potential of urine therapy, suggesting that certain components may help alleviate inflammation. This aligns with historical uses of urine therapy for conditions ranging from skin disorders to joint inflammation.

Historical Roots of Urine Therapy

Ancient Civilizations

The roots of urine therapy trace back to ancient civilizations, with evidence of its practice found in Egyptian, Jewish, Greek, and Roman cultures. In these societies, urine was regarded not only as a waste product but also as a substance with potential healing properties.

Middle Ages and Renaissance

During the Middle Ages and Renaissance, urine therapy experienced a resurgence in popularity, notably in Europe. Physicians of the time used urine as a diagnostic tool and therapeutic agent. Swiss physician Paracelsus, a prominent figure during the Renaissance, advocated for urine therapy and believed in its potential to treat various ailments.

18th Century Onward

The 18th century witnessed a continuation of urine therapy, with proponents emphasizing its holistic benefits. While it fell out of favor with the rise of modern medicine and scientific advancements, urine therapy persisted on the fringes of alternative medicine.

Contemporary Practice

In contemporary times, urine therapy has found a niche among alternative health enthusiasts. The practice persists, with individuals attributing diverse health benefits to the consumption or application of their own urine. Its enduring presence reflects a continued curiosity and openness to alternative wellness practices.

Conclusion

Urine therapy, deeply entrenched in Indian culture and woven into the fabric of diverse civilizations, continues to spark interest and debate. Scientifically, urine therapy's potential lies in its composition, featuring antibacterial, immunological, hormonal, and anti-inflammatory components. As we unravel the historical tapestry of urine therapy, its journey through time reveals a persistent thread connecting ancient civilizations to the modern era. While the scientific community may remain skeptical, the enduring practice of urine therapy invites further exploration and consideration.

4
HOW I DISCOVERED URINE THERAPY

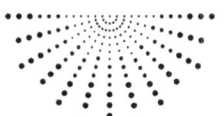

*D*uring the pandemic I was seeking out how we could best help to restore a persons DNA from the Covid Vaccination. It was clear that these shots were harmful to many and deadly to some. No matter what, no matter where, we needed to find a solution that was readily available and with little to no cost so that the masses could resort to if needed. As an advanced holistic practitioner, I saw the scans of hundreds of clients post the vaccination. I literally thought my scanner was broken as everyone was showing up with the same kinds of issues. These included but not limited to AIDS, HIV, Cancer, Myocarditis and Snake Venom. With months of research, my findings were true. True to the point they existed within the DNA of my own daughter. She had felt pressured to get the shot as she was limited access to grocery stores, public transportation and more without it. As any mom would be, I was devastated but also didn't want to worry her for her decision. I am a solutions person and focus on how to resolve the problem at hand, knowing the answer is out there, if I just look hard enough.

As news leaked out of young athletes dropping dead, reporters and newscasters dropping dead, etc., I also heard of a variety of solutions that were helpful. These reporting where not mainstream news, nonetheless but they were solutions that were proving effective to those suffering from COVID and the shots that followed. One such solution aside from Ivermectin, was the nicotine patch. But beyond that, Urine therapy stood out as a solution to help restore ones very own DNA. Something that was altered, (I say intentionally).

I was quite surprised with my research to discover many other countries already knew the benefits of Urine Therapy. Something that is always available, completely free and effective based on my own personal experience, and the hundreds of clients I have witnessed who were open to try it. This was exciting to me but also a challenge, for I am not one to just recommend to anyone before trying it out for myself.

My First Attempt.

That very next week, I was traveling to Florida. I absolutely love the ocean and spent considerable amount of time enjoying being in the water. There were several opportunities that arose during my time there, to allow me to try some of the applications of urine therapy out on myself. Because I spend so much time swimming and playing in the ocean waters, after the third day, I felt an ear infection coming on. I could tell I had water in the ear and began to feel a dull pain developing. This is when I remembered…URINE THERAPY!

I literally peed on my finger and dropped several drops into my ear. I did this every time I went pee. The very next day I felt better. I was astonished!

The second thing that happened was because I sat around in a wet bathing suit in the hot sun, I felt a yeast infection coming on. I again remembered Urine Therapy. As I would urinate in the toilet, I put two fingers into the flow of the stream and pushed it up inside my vagina, and running it along the vaginal walls. Each time I went to the bathroom I repeated this method. My thick creamy yeast infection was getting diluted with each application. It instantly helped calm the itchy feeling and smell. Two days of that and my vagina was back in balance and feeling fresh and happy.

During the flight back home, my left eye was feeling blurry. I saw from my scan I had bacteria and I could have simply used rife technology to eliminate the bacteria, but again I remembered Urine Therapy. At my first opportunity I peed on my finger and dropped 1 drop of urine in my eye. I definitely was more reluctant because I was afraid of stinging and more afraid of making my eye worse. But to my surprise, it cleared immediately!

Continuing my exploration with this new concept, I knew I had a way to go. My skin was dry and red from the Florida sun. This is where I decided to bathe with urine. Instead of stepping out to avoid peeing in the water, I purposely allowed my pee to fill in with the bath water, essential oils and Epsom Salt. Sounds pretty crazy to do this and want to feel and smell clean right? Well, we are immersed for 9 months in our own urine while in the womb and come out super soft and protected.

Constipation has always been a challenge for me especially when I travel. To me this method of using urine as an enema was not a big deal. Our anal canal accesses a point where it reaches the entirety of our body. To do a urine enema is quite easy because if you feel urine is dirty, then to put it up another dirty area doesn't feel that bad. Not only does it help with constipation, but the benefits are shared throughout the body reaching areas where the other methods cannot.

I have yet to sniff or snort urine as a way to open up my sinuses. I haven't really needed to go there. Just like we use the Nettepot, you can use urine in the same way.

Last but not least is the dreaded….OMG, I need to drink this stuff. Personally, I wanted to see if I could. How was it, how did it taste, etc. I have read enough on the subject to know that it doesn't have to be the first urine. I have tried the first urine and it was super salty and had a very nutty aftertaste. I held my breath and gulped about 1 cup of it, chasing it with some juice. It immediately gave me energy. I already have good energy but this was noticeable.

Today, I will typically drink my 2nd or 3rd urine. I am overall healthy and looking to continue to improve my health, reduce abnormal cell growth (cancer cells) and eliminate pathogens which are so prevalent these days from our air, water and food. I even use it in my smoothies from time to time. You won't even notice the difference in taste. Typically anything after your first urine, it will be light yellow in color and no smell. I like to store some in the fridge for later use. It just gets me worked up to drink hot or warm pee. So I have figured out what works for me. If I feel like I am coming down with something, I would definitely turn to ingesting urine.

So there you have it. That is how I personally have discovered it. Some benefits I have seen for myself is that it balances hormones, releases weight, helps with anti-aging (by applying on the face and neck) and can help with burns, cuts, and bug bites. It has been amazing to hear the many miracles of my clients who are faced with life threatening illnesses and how these methods have reversed their symptoms and set them on a life of health and wellness.

5
COMPOSITION OF URINE

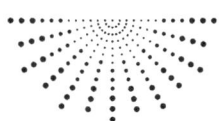

The human body produces and excretes urine, a liquid waste product. Renal tubules produce this substance, which then collects in the urine bladder before being passed out of the body via the urethra. Although water accounts for 91% to 96% of its mass, many other solid and liquid elements are also present.

Urine is a bodily waste product that contains salt, water, and other substances. Regular urination is necessary to prevent harmful buildup in the body. Urinary tract infections and bladder atrophy, which can cause incontinence, can develop if urine is not passed. A burst bladder can occur in extremely unusual circumstances when a person holds their urine for an extended period of time. Urine retention seldom results in mortality because the body will release it on its own; nevertheless, if the bladder bursts from retention for an extended period of time, it can be fatal and requires emergency medical intervention.

Several indicators of health can be gleaned by analyzing a person's urine.

Color - Normal human urine ranges from a pale yellow to rich amber. Beets are one food that has been shown to alter the color of urine.

Smell - Urine that is otherwise healthy does not have much of a smell. If a person is dehydrated, the odor of ammonia may be more pronounced. The smell can also be altered by consuming certain foods or experiencing certain medical conditions.

PH - A substance's acidity or basicity can be described by its pH level. The pH variation in urine is the widest of any body fluid. Normal urine has a pH between 4.5 and 8.

Density - Urine density is affected by the total quantity of dissolved chemicals present. Electrolytes and waste products are two examples of such substances. Urine density is also significantly affected by the availability of surplus water. Specific gravity of typical human urine is ranged at 1.003 to 1.030.

Toxicity - Urine itself is not usually harmful, but the germs and pathogens in it can be. It's vulnerable to infection from bacteria and other infections.

You may be asking, what then, does urine consist of? It contains water, which accounts for around 95% of Urine, is the most abundant component on earth and in the body. The concentration of an animal's urine is proportional to the amount of water it drinks. This occurs because urine only contains water that has been urinated out. Urine also contains waste items that must be eliminated from the body.

Creatinine is another urinalysis-detected metabolic byproduct. The kidneys process creatinine, a byproduct of muscular contractions, and expel it in the urine. It accounts for about 0.1% of the urine's total volume. The electrolytes chloride, sodium, and potassium make up a significant portion of urine's overall composition.

Pigments can also be found in urine. Urine's pigments give it its typical variety of colors, from pale yellow to deep amber. Urochrome, urobilin, and uroerythrin are the primary pigments in urine. Urine is a major route for hormone elimination. Medical testing can identify certain hormones, which can then be used to determine diagnosis. Amino acids and metabolites are also found in urine.

Over ninety-nine percent of all solutes in urine have concentrations of 10 mg/L or more, and these 68 compounds account for almost all of them. There are a total of 42 chemicals at play here. The following categories can be used to describe them:

- Electrolytes such as sodium, potassium, calcium, magnesium and chloride
- Nitrogenous chemicals such as urea and creatinine
- Vitamins
- Hormones
- Organic acids such as uric acid
- Other organic compounds

Urine is an ultra-filtrate of the plasma that is constantly being formed by the kidneys. The average daily urine output of 1200mL is the result of reabsorbing the water and filtered chemicals required to physiological function, which comes from a volume of around 170,000 mL of filtered plasma.

Approximately 95% of urine is water, whereas the remaining 5% contains various solutes.

- Urea.
- Organic substances like creatinine and uric acid.
- Inorganic substances. The major substance is chloride (CL^-), followed by Na+ and K+.
- The dietary intake makes it difficult to decide on the normal level.
- Water.

Other substances found are:

- Hormones.
- Drugs.
- Vitamins.
- Cells.

- Cast.
- Crystals
- Bacteria.

BENEFITS OF THE VARIOUS COMPONENTS OF URINE

- Urea

This byproduct is produced when proteins are broken down. In all mammals and some fishes, urea is the primary nitrogenous waste product from the breakdown of protein in the metabolic process. Mammals excrete it in their urine, as well as their blood, bile, milk, and sweat.

Urea is used as a fertilizer, feed additive, and intermediate in the production of polymers and pharmaceuticals, among other things. It is a colorless, crystalline substance that melts around 132.7 degrees Celsius (271 degrees Fahrenheit) and breaks down before it boils.

Natural moisturizing factor (NMF) is an essential component of a well-hydrated skin barrier, and urea is a key component of NMF. Urea has a unique combination of hydrating and exfoliating effects, making it a popular ingredient in body cleansers and moisturizers. This component, when used in sufficient quantity, acts as a keratolytic agent, clearing away excess layers of dead skin. Urea has been shown to alleviate the signs of dry, rough, or scaly skin when used topically as part of a regular skincare routine.

Numerous body washes, lotions, and creams contain urea because of its moisturizing characteristics and ability to help remove extra dead skin cells. Psoriasis and eczema are two skin disorders that can cause dry, flaky, itchy, and scaly skin, and urea-based skincare solutions are commonly formulated to alleviate these symptoms.

- Creatinine:

This byproduct is produced when muscle tissue is broken down. What this means is that creatinine is a byproduct of the regular breakdown of muscle tissue in the body. There is creatinine in the blood of everyone.

Creatinine helps your muscles by providing them with fuel. About half is obtained by eating, with the remainder being manufactured by the liver and kidneys. Creatinine is a substance that many athletes use to get stronger and perform better. When taken by otherwise healthy adults, supplements pose no risk.

Creatinine is a naturally occurring molecule in the body that provides energy for muscular contractions. The Greek term for "meat" is whence this dish gets its name. The liver and kidneys create roughly half of the body's supply, while the remaining half is transported to the skeletal muscles for usage. The vast majority of your body's creatinine supply is kept in skeletal muscle for use when you're working out. By keeping production high in active muscles, creatinine helps ensure that working muscles never run out of fuel. Your heart, brain, and other tissues contain trace quantities as well.

Foods like milk, red meat, and seafood all contain creatinine. Creatinine intake averages 1-2 grams daily on a balanced omnivore/carnivore diet. Creatinine levels may be decreased in vegetarians and vegans.

Creatinine and the related chemical creatinine, which is used as a diagnostic indicator of renal health, coexist in the body. The urine is the means by which it leaves the body. This implies that, depending on your muscle mass, your body will need to release some of its stored creatinine every day in order to maintain steady levels. Creatinine is produced naturally in the body, but maintaining enough amounts requires including it in your regular diet.

Creatinine supplements have been used by athletes of all skill levels and professions to enhance performance and surined recovery from training. Creatinine boosts performance by increasing "quick burst" energy and strength but has minimal impact on aerobic endurance. Male athletes that participate in power sports like football, wrestling, hockey, and bodybuilding are the most common consumers of Creatinine supplements.

- Uric acid

One of the byproducts of purine metabolism

The breakdown of proteins produces ammonia. Uric acid, then, is a byproduct of blood metabolism. The breakdown of purines in the body results in its formation. The majority of uric acid is eliminated from the body in urine after dissolving in the blood.

When we look at the uric acid levels in people's blood, we see hyperuricemia, which can lead to gout. Numerous epidemiological studies have established a link between uric acid and a variety of diseases and conditions, including overweight and obesity, metabolic syndrome, high blood pressure, and heart disease. Researchers and doctors have long known that the content of uric acid in the blood is a crucial indicator of the course of many complex diseases.

Drugs that lower uric acid levels can lessen the severity of gout attacks, slow the development of tophi, and prevent further joint damage.

- Electrolytes

Electrolytes such as sodium, potassium, and chloride ions, play a role in maintaining proper fluid balance in the body. Substances that, when dissolved in water, form ions and acquire the ability to conduct electricity are known as electrolytes. The human body contains electrolytes, and maintaining a healthy electrolyte balance is critical to cellular and organ health.

HOW URINE THERAPY WORKS IN THE BODY

Urine consumption, in whatever form it takes, has deep historical roots. urine therapy, urophagia, or urotherapy are modern terms for the historical practice of using urine for medical purposes.

The treatment of many diseases, from acne to cancer, with urine therapy has been documented as far back as ancient Rome, Greece, and Egypt. At one time, doctors used a taste test to determine whether or not a patient had diabetes.

Nowadays, people make similarly expansive claims about the healing possibilities of urine. If you are reading this book and thinking, should you urinate in your morning smoothie or should you just drink it straight? Most likely not.

Below, however, are some of the proposed mechanisms by which urine treatment may exert its beneficial effects.

1. Through nutrient re-absorption and reutilization

Most of the time, the body can get what it needs nutritionally just by eating. Many of the vitamins, amino acids, minerals, hormones, etc. that are present in urine can be reabsorbed and utilised again if the urine is consumed or massaged into the skin.

This is especially crucial when sick bodily tissue is circulating in the blood and needs to be flushed out of the body. After passing through the kidneys' filtering process, this tissue should be broken down to its original materials and utilised by the body to construct new tissue.

During disease, the kidneys filter out vital substances that never made it to their destination. This alters the urine's chemical makeup. Hepatitis (liver inflammation) is a common complication of liver obstruction. If the liver's bile ducts get blocked, the bile the liver produces leaks into the bloodstream and eventually the urine, causing fatigue and nausea. Lack of bile in the digestive system makes it difficult to break down fats and proteins. Therefore, it is common practice to recommend bed rest and a diet low in fat and protein.

However, the molecule that should break down these proteins and lipids is present in urine at the correct concentration. In this view, bile and other liver enzymes can be recycled through the use of urine treatment.

This is just one disease in which the excreted urine can be put to good use. Research into the storage and reuse of vital physiological substances could also be used to the study of other diseases.

1. Through Re-absorption of hormones

Hormones re-absorbed from urine when taken orally are primarily the tiny ones that are not proteins (protein-complexes), as the proteins are broken down by the acids, pepsins, and enzymes in the digestive system. More study is needed to determine the long-term effects of re-absorbing sex hormones, adrenal gland hormones, and thyroid hormones. Hormones can be safely reabsorbed through the skin after being applied to the outside of the body in the form of urine. Since urine is absorbed directly into the tissue, massaging with urine is an important supplementary component of urine therapy. In addition to aiding in the treatment of allergic illnesses, enemas can prevent the breakdown of some hormones by gastric acids. Injecting urine has the same effect.

Two important contexts call for re-absorption. Firstly certain hormones have a very specific effect during a healing process. For instance, cortico-steroids, which are secreted by the adrenal cortex, help treat inflammatory diseases like rheumatism and asthma, as well as allergies like hay fever and eczema. It has not yet been shown that these hormones play a role in the treatment, but auto-urine therapy has proven to be an incredibly effective assistance in the treatment of all these ailments.

Second, re-absorption can help the body save energy in other ways. The body can save energy by reusing hormones that have been previously ingested rather than producing entirely new hormones.

Hormones are very potent chemicals, and their manufacturing expends a lot of energy. When even a small number of these molecules are released, they can completely disrupt the equilibrium of biological processes, the personality, the emotions, and the state of mind. The re-absorption of even a small amount of hormones may therefore have a significant impact on our health and vitality.

1. Through Involvement of the Immune System

Urine is not poisonous, but it may contain trace levels of toxins if the person is sick. This minute remnant of metabolites may be one reason why urine treatment works so well. The immune system is activated if certain substances enter the body and set off an immunological response. This is why urine therapy has been so effective in treating allergies; if compounds that leave the body via the urine are the same as those engaged in the sickness process, they can activate the defense system to attack.

Vaccinations work in a similar way, by introducing even trace amounts of potentially harmful chemicals into an otherwise healthy body. This may have homeopathic or isopathic effects, as it causes the immune system to produce antibodies (and hence defend the body). Urine therapy, which includes ingesting and massaging with urine, is thought to boost immunity by providing antibodies with easier access to the body. We have already speculated about the potential role of urea and glutamine in the immune system

1. Through Bactericidal and virucidal effect

The exact mechanism through which urea contributes to urine's germicidal and antiseptic properties is still under investigation. The cleansing properties of ammonia are comparable to those of salt. Urine has antimicrobial and fungicidal properties in addition to its ability to kill bacteria. Both urea and ammonia have been shown to have a potent anti-viral effect in studies.

Urine's antibacterial and anti-fly properties make it a useful first aid treatment for minor cuts and scrapes, especially in warmer climates. Compresses made of either fresh or old urine are effective in fighting illnesses and clearing them up. Externally applied urine has a potent antiseptic effect, although it cannot completely stop the growth of germs in the urethra (infections still occur).

1. Through the use of Detoxification
   Treatment

In some (fasting) treatments, drinking salt water is an essential part of the treatment. When used in yoga, salt water helps cleanse the body from the inside out, relieving symptoms of asthma, stomach ulcer, indigestion, and constipation. Urine, like table salt, has the same effect when ingested. This may be a major factor in the treatment's efficacy.

Mucous membranes can be cleansed of built-up gunk with the help of a salt solution. Ingesting a salty liquid allows some of the salt to enter the body, where it can help break down excess mucus in the respiratory system and elsewhere.

Experts in this field claim that warm salt water, and by extension, fresh warm urine, is most beneficial for patients suffering from conditions in which the body is unable to create enough heat to keep typical physiological secretions thin and watery. As an added bonus, urine helps eliminate fluid retention caused by illness. This also explains the beneficial effects of applying compresses made of warm, concentrated urine to the skin.

Using urine for constipation relief is recommended due to its laxative properties, as it is a salty liquid that attracts water and dissolves waste as it moves through the digestive system. This facilitates the passing of stool.

There is a hypothesis that consuming urine has a similar effect on the body's metabolism as drinking salt water, helping to eliminate sugar from the bloodstream and toxins from the body. Urine therapy is an effective method of purification.

Advocates of urine therapy suggest that the natural cortisone found in urine gives it an advantage over salt water. This is due to the hormone-related effects of urination.

Urine is a superior alternative to salt water because urea and ammonia are organic solvents that break down lipids and other bodily secretions. These chemicals likely have a profound effect on the mucosal membranes and cells of the body.

Urine therapy has implications beyond the individual level for modern medicine, challenging the idea that complex theories and technologies are necessary for good health. Instead, it suggests that the body and the world have limitless potential.

Urine therapy allows us to tap into a powerful internal healer that operates on both the physical and energetic planes. This idea suggests that urine, as a holographic material, can influence not just the physical, but also the electromagnetic fields of emotions and the intellect, and even the subtler genetic vibrational information of the soul.

6
PREPARING FOR URINE THERAPY

*U*rine therapy, an ancient and controversial practice, involves the use of one's urine for medicinal purposes. This alternative medical treatment involves drinking urine, applying it topically to the skin, or even using it in a nasal rinse. While the idea of using urine for healing may seem repulsive to many people, the use of urine as medicine dates back to ancient times.

Historically, many cultures have used urine for medicinal purposes. For instance, the ancient Egyptians, Chinese, Indians, Aztecs, and Romans all utilized urine in a variety of medicinal applications, including wound healing, teeth whitening, and even as an antiseptic. Urine was also used in traditional medicine systems such as Ayurveda, where it was believed to have therapeutic properties.

Despite the lack of scientific evidence, urine therapy has gained popularity in recent years, particularly in alternative medicine circles. Proponents of urine therapy claim that it can cure a wide range of health issues, from acne to cancer, and even HIV/AIDS.

While the use of urine for medicinal purposes has been practiced for centuries, and those who have tried it can share about its effectiveness in curing illnesses.

DISPELLING THE MYTHS ASSOCIATED WITH URINE

A phobia of urineing that is both irrational and learned. The following types of prejudice should be eradicated:

- Urine is ripe with microorganisms.

Paruresis, also known as shy bladder syndrome, is a condition where an individual has difficulty urinating in public or in the presence of others. This phobia is both irrational and learned, and it can be debilitating for those who suffer from it. People with paruresis may avoid drinking fluids in order to avoid having to use public restrooms, or they may choose to hold their urine for long periods of time, which can lead to urinary tract infections and other complications.

One of the common misconceptions about urine is that it is ripe with microorganisms that can cause infections. However, within the first fifteen minutes after it exits the body, the urine of the person who produced it poses no risk of infection to anyone else. While it is true that urine can contain bacteria, viruses, and other microorganisms, they need time to incubate in order to pose a threat to health. In fact, urine can even be helpful in certain situations, such as treating a jellyfish sting or relieving the pain of a toothache.

- Urine smells

Urine doesn't start to smell until the uric acid in it turns into ammonia, which takes some time. Until then, it's odorless. However, if the urine is absorbed via the skin or if it is used within the home, such as on window glass, and then thoroughly washed off later, the stench will be completely eliminated.

In order to eliminate these prejudices and misconceptions about urine, it is important to educate people about the properties of urine and its uses in different contexts. By understanding the science behind urine, people can overcome their fears and phobias and use this resource in a safe and hygienic manner.

- Urine is a waste product

To put back into the body a fluid that it has just finished exerting so much effort to flush out is contrary to common sense. The answer is as simple and straightforward as this: Urine, much like each of our distinct personalities, is a storehouse of all the many experiences that our bodies have had throughout our lives. Urine is a storehouse of information regarding allergies, infections, and diseases as well as disturbances. By providing the immune system with this information once more, we can facilitate the (hopefully) expeditious creation of a defense mechanism.

Therefore, the immune system acquires knowledge from urine in this way.

In fact, everything that is in the front of the body is pure. Such as our saliva, our breast milk, semen, blood from menstruation and our urine!

- Urine develops an unpleasant odor on the skin

On the contrary, this is true. Having said that, it is necessary for the fluid to be absorbed entirely. Compresses, for example, should be produced from an animal fiber such as wool rather than cotton since, as we all know from wearing cotton diapers, urine quickly creates an unpleasant odor in cotton, and this is something that should be avoided at all costs. Urine should never be used to clean synthetic fibers in any circumstance.

- Urine is known to carry harmful bacteria and viruses.

Because the liver has already removed them, our urine does not contain any viruses or bacteria that could be dangerous because the liver has already filtered them out. The ones that are still there are the ones that the body can conquer with the help of urine treatment.

- Urine tastes horrible

A healthy person's first urine of the day will always have a salty and bitter taste to it, just like other urine. However, rather than making its way through the capillaries of the tongue, this flavor will go directly to the nose. If you drink with your nose covered while drinking, you won't be able to taste anything at all. If you avoid dairy and meat the urine will not have any bitter taste. As the glass is full of pale urine, no smell and literally no taste but a slight nutty aftertaste.

- Rashes that occur on a baby's bottom are caused by urine.

It is a common misconception that urine is the cause of rashes on a baby's bottom. In reality, this is completely false and serves only to benefit the diaper industry. The truth is that the buttocks of a baby are not particularly susceptible to the effects of urine. Rather, the main culprit behind diaper rash is often the food that the nursing mother or the infant is eating. Certain foods, such as citrus fruits or acidic foods, can cause irritation and inflammation on the skin, leading to a rash.

Other factors that can contribute to diaper rash include prolonged exposure to wetness, friction from diapers, and not changing the diaper frequently enough. It is important to maintain good hygiene practices and to change the baby's diaper frequently to prevent diaper rash from developing. If a rash does occur, there are various creams and ointments available that can help to soothe and heal the affected area.

It is important to dispel this myth about urine causing diaper rash, as it can lead to unnecessary worry and fear among new parents. By understanding the true causes of diaper rash and taking appropriate preventative measures, parents can help to keep their baby's bottom healthy and rash-free.

In the event that you have stumbled into this chapter while looking for information on the collection and preservation of urine for therapeutic purposes, you should be aware that it is as easy as collecting urine samples.

HOW TO COLLECT & STORE URINE FOR THERAPY

Inquire about the procedure and get answers from a qualified urine specialist. Find out if there are any foods you should avoid before, during, and after collecting your urine.

This is the standard procedure for collecting and storing urine for therapeutic purposes:

Urine can be collected in a glass jar or jug. To store the urine, you can transfer it from the collection container to another one. You can should refrigerate it or store it in the sun or in a dark area. There really is no right or wrong here. You can even have a cheesecloth over the opening to let the fumes out in the sun or have it closed off.

When you urinate, the clock starts ticking on the 24-hour collection. However, it is possible that your urine specialist will inform you when to begin. Early am is a usual time to begin collecting. Urine samples should be collected throughout the next 24 hours.

Some feel urine from your first urination session should not be saved. Others swear by it. This book is an introduction and you should do your own research to feel what is right for you.

HYGIENE PRACTICES FOR URINE THERAPY: IS URINE STERILE

Urine normally only includes minute amounts of bacteria and other pathogens. However, many people are under the impression that urine is sterile, which is not the case. When something is sterile, it is perfectly clean in every manner; there is not even the slightest trace of dirt or bacteria left behind.

Bacterial colonies can be found both within and on the outside of our bodies, and they contribute to our overall health and well-being. This suggests that our bladder, like the rest of our body, is not entirely free of pathogens.

It is well knowledge that a high bacterial load is connected to infections of the urinary system. On the other hand, a growing body of research has identified various species of helpful bacteria that live in the bladder and are expelled from the body in the urine of healthy persons. These bacteria are thought to have a role in preventing urinary tract infections.

ARE THERE HEALTH BENEFITS TO DRINKING URINE?

Urine is one of the substances that may be obtained absolutely free of charge virtually anywhere. Everyone urinates a little bit here and there during the day. Urine, because of its easy availability, has been incorporated into a wide variety of traditional medicinal practices throughout the world to treat a variety of diseases and conditions. Urine has a rich history of use as a home remedy, particularly for the following conditions:

- Arthritis
- Allergies
- Cancer
- Indigestion
- Migraines
- Infertility

7

INTERNAL URINE THERAPY

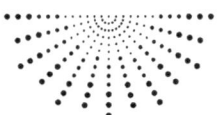

*I*nternal urine therapy, which involves drinking one's own urine, has been practiced for a very long time in many different cultures all over the world. It has been connected to a number of benefits to health, including those associated with digestion, the immune system, inflammation, and energy levels. However, proponents of Internal urine Therapy assert that it is a risk-free and effective method for enhancing one's health, despite the fact that many individuals find the idea of ingesting urine to be revolting.

The majority of urine's complex liquid composition is made up of water, electrolytes, and waste materials. Urine is a complex liquid. It is made up of a large number of different components, some of which include hormones, enzymes, and antibodies. Some of these chemicals have a variety of potential therapeutic applications, including anti-inflammatory and antibacterial activities, to name just two of those applications. Urine, for example, is known to contain the chemical urea, which has traditionally been utilized in the treatment of skin conditions such as eczema and psoriasis. Your own urine contains a significant amount of the vitamins and minerals that are necessary for you to live in the best possible condition.

Proponents of Internal urine Therapy contend that ingesting one's own urine can facilitate the body's natural detoxification process and boost one's immune system. They contend that urine is the body's natural way of getting rid of waste and that reintroducing it can help to activate the body's own healing mechanisms. This argument is based on the fact that urine is the body's natural way of getting rid of waste.

DRINKING URINE FOR INTERNAL THERAPY

The practice of collecting one's own urine and drinking it, either undiluted or after being diluted with water, is referred to as "drinking urine for internal therapy." It is recommended to consume the urine as soon as it is collected or to refrigerate it for later use; therefore, ensure that the container you use to collect it is clean. It is better to start off slowly with a modest dose and gradually increase it from there. While some people prefer to do it first thing in the morning when they wake up, others find it more convenient to do it before they eat.

On the other hand, not all urine is intended for ingestion by humans. It is believed that urine collected first thing in the morning contains the highest concentration of therapeutic compounds, making it the most effective for internal therapy. It is essential to consume a large amount of water throughout the day since doing so enables the body to eliminate toxins and maintain proper hydration levels.

Internal urination therapy has been reported to have a good impact on the health of a large number of persons. The following are some of the benefits that are most frequently cited by supporters:

Aiding digestion The process of digestion can be improved thanks to the enzymes and other chemicals that are present in urine. The use of this may be beneficial for a variety of digestive conditions, including bloating, acid reflux, and constipation, to name just a few.

Urine possesses antibacterial and antiviral capabilities as a result of the antibodies and other substances that are present in it. Urine is produced by the kidneys. People who have a compromised immune system or who experience frequent bouts of illness are likely to benefit the most from this.

Urine contains compounds that have anti-inflammatory properties and can help reduce inflammation throughout the body. Inflammatory diseases such as arthritis, asthma, and allergies are some of the conditions that may be helped by therapy.

Because of its anti-inflammatory qualities, urea found in urine has been shown to alleviate skin conditions such as eczema, psoriasis, and acne. As a result of its capacity to heal wounds and retain moisture, it is beneficial to the skin.

Urine contains an assortment of the vitamins and minerals that are important for optimal health and can contribute to an increase in one's level of energy. It may be of considerable value to people who suffer from chronic fatigue syndrome or other disorders that cause comparable symptoms, such as feeling weary all the time.

How to Practice Internal Urine Therapy

In order to put Internal urine Therapy into practice, urine must be collected and then consumed, either undiluted or after being diluted with water. Urine ought to be collected in a sanitary container and either used immediately or stored in the refrigerator for later consumption. It is better to start off slowly with a modest dose and gradually increase it from there. While some people prefer to do it first thing in the morning when they wake up, others find it more convenient to do it before they eat.

Internal Urine Therapy is not a one-size-fits-all solution; nevertheless, there are a number of recommended practices that can assist in making it as safe and successful as is humanly possible. If, for example, you drink water on a consistent basis throughout the day, you can avoid toxins as well as becoming dehydrated. It is recommended that you stay away from processed meals, alcoholic beverages, and caffeine as much as possible because these things can hinder the body's ability to heal itself.

DOSAGES AND FREQUENCIES FOR URINE THERAPY

The dosage of urine therapy administered to each individual should be individualized to take into account their particular ailment, age range, and overall health. It is preferable to begin treatment with a low dose and gradually increase it over time. This will help lessen the likelihood of adverse reactions occurring. It's possible that proponents of urine therapy are onto something, but it's still a good idea to take things slowly and make sure you're following all of the guidelines.

Dosages for the Urine Therapy

The recommended amounts of urine treatment vary depending on a person's age and their current state of health. It is common advice to start with a very little quantity, such as a few drops or a teaspoon, then gradually increase the amount taken over time. Drinking less water than an adult would, typically between 2 and 6 ounces per day, is appropriate for children.

The quality of the urine may also have an impact on the appropriate dosage. When treating with urine that is either diluted or of inferior quality, it is possible that a higher dose will be required to achieve the same desired therapeutic effect.

Frequencies for Urine Therapy

Depending on the patient's condition and the patient's overall health status, urine therapy may be delivered on a weekly, biweekly, or monthly basis. Urine is something that some people like to drink on a consistent basis, while for others it may be something they only do sometimes or when necessary.

The frequency of urine therapy should be adjusted based on how the body reacts to the treatment. Consuming big volumes or consistent doses of urine might make some people feel sick to their stomachs and cause them to vomit. In certain circumstances, the urine therapy may require certain modifications, either in terms of the frequency of administration or the dosage.

8

EXTERNAL URINE THERAPY

The process of applying urine to an external surface, such as the skin, hair, or nails, is referred to as external urine therapy. Many people believe that external urine therapy can enhance the health of the skin as well as the health of the body as a whole, despite the unconventional character of this treatment.

Urine from humans has the potential to improve a variety of physical and mental health conditions. Mixing powdered potato and sulphur with hot, stale urine is an effective treatment for preventing hair loss. It has been demonstrated that reducing hair loss can be accomplished by massaging this mixture into the scalp. It is recommended to gargle with urine to which a little saffron has been added in order to alleviate any and all sorts of throat discomfort. Trembling hands and knees can be alleviated by washing the affected areas with warm urine and then pressing the urine into the skin shortly after urinating. If you start each day with a glass of your own water for nine consecutive days, not only will you be healed of scurvy but you will also feel significantly better overall. It is beneficial for alcoholic jaundice as well as dropsy. Earaches can be alleviated and protection against noise-induced hearing loss can be provided by drinking warm water from the bottle. In the event that your eyes are bothersome, rinsing them with water from the same source will assist ease the pain and improve your eyesight.

Washing and rubbing the hands with it can help eliminate numbness, chaps, and sores, as well as enhance flexibility in the muscles and joints. Any kind of green wound that you want to wash with it will be miraculously cured if you use it. The itching sensation will go away if you scratch whatever it is and then wash it. Urine therapy is the paradigmatic example of the fundamental principles that underlie alternative medical practice. A one-of-a-kind treatment is using the urine that comes from the sick individual themself. Because its component parts are continuously changing, it is always able to conform to the preferences and requirements of the individual.

APPLYING URINE TOPICALLY FOR EXTERNAL THERAPY

External urine therapy, also known as urethral therapy, is the process of applying freshly urinated urine to various parts of the body, including the skin, the hair, and the nails, with the goal of enhancing overall health and well-being. The method, which has been used for centuries in traditional medical practices such as Ayurveda and traditional Chinese medicine, may strike some people as odd, yet it has a lengthy history of application.

Amaroli, also known as urine therapy, is a form of yoga that is conducted in accordance with Ayurveda. Urine, according to practitioners of the Amaroli tradition, is a powerful medicinal agent that can assist in the cleansing of the body and the balance of the doshas (the energy systems that make up the body). Urine therapy, also known as Shudan in Chinese medicine, is employed in the treatment of a broad variety of diseases, including conditions associated with the digestive system, the lungs, and the skin.

One of the primary advantages of using external urine therapy is that it has the potential to improve the health of the skin. Urine contains urea, which functions as a natural exfoliant, helping to clear out pores and reduce acne. Urea has a number of other benefits, including the ability to moisturize the skin and even out its tone and texture. Because of its naturally occurring antibacterial properties, urine may also help prevent infections and hasten the healing of wounds.

There is a possibility that urine therapy will also be beneficial to the hair and nails. According to the findings of several studies, the proteins and minerals included in urine have the potential to stimulate hair growth and improve the health of the scalp and hair. Urine can be used to protect against nail fungus and to prevent the weakening of nails.

However, when applied to the skin in this manner, urine should be handled with extreme caution. Incorrect collection or utilization of urine can put patients at risk for contamination and infection. These risks can be minimized or eliminated entirely by collecting and using fresh urine in the appropriate manner. It is standard custom to dilute urine with water in order to reduce the offensive smell of the urine and to make it more tolerable to apply to the skin.

Before using it on a larger scale, it is possible to test a tiny patch of skin with urine to determine whether or not it causes any allergic reactions or skin sensitivities. In addition to this, it is a good idea to clean the area around where you urinate with some soap and water both before and after you urinate.

It is essential to be aware of the potential risks associated with external urination therapy, even if there are no known serious side effects associated with it. There is a possibility that some individuals will have momentary skin irritation or a burning sensation; however, this is quickly rectified by washing the affected area with soap and water. In the event that you experience any unpleasant reactions or infections, it is essential that you seek medical attention.

In conclusion, external urine therapy is a tried-and-true way of treatment that is integrated into the practice of traditional medicine in many parts of the world. The potential benefits for the skin, hair, and nails cannot outweigh the requirement to exercise caution and to collect and apply the substance in the appropriate manner. Before beginning any alternative health practice, you should discuss it with your primary care physician, particularly if you have a medical problem or use medication for it.

VARIOUS METHODS FOR APPLYING URINE EXTERNALLY

External urine therapy, also known as urethral therapy, is the practice of applying urine to the skin, hair, or nails with the intention of promoting the body's natural healing processes and improving overall health. When applied to the skin, urine can have a number of different effects, depending on the specific application method.

Direct Application:

Urine is taken, and it is then applied topically to the skin or the scalp. It is recommended that a tiny volume of urine be collected in a container, and then either a cotton ball or a towel be used to apply the urine. This method is effective in treating a wide variety of skin conditions, including some of the more common ones including acne, eczema, and psoriasis.

Urine Compress:

To make a urine compress, first you soak a bandage or cloth in fresh urine, then you put the urine-soaked bandage or cloth to the area that is hurt. To accomplish this, simply saturate a clean towel in fresh urine and squeeze away the excess water. After you have secured the compress in place by wrapping it in plastic wrap or a bandage, you should apply it to the area that was injured. This medication is typically effective for inflammatory illnesses such joint pain, muscle soreness, and headaches.

Urine Massage:

It is believed that massaging an injured area with fresh urine will hasten the healing process and boost blood flow to the area that is being massaged. When applying fresh urine to the skin or the scalp, it is best to do it using a circular motion. This method is extensively used for the purpose of enhancing the health of the skin, increasing its firmness, and promoting the growth of hair.

Urine Soak:

It has been demonstrated that adding urine to a bath or foot soak can have significant benefits on relaxation as well as the health of the skin. To accomplish this, simply add one cup of fresh urine to a warm bath or foot soak and then soak for a few minutes. This method is applied frequently due to the relaxing qualities it imparts as well as the positive impact it has on the skin.

Urine Spray:

Urine spray can be applied to the skin or hair by first diluting fresh urine with water and then using a spray bottle to apply the mixture. To accomplish this, shake one cup of urine into a spray bottle that has been filled with water. The next step is to spray the solution straight onto the skin or hair, and then wait for it to dry. The most common use include treating dry skin, stimulating hair growth, and neutralizing unpleasant body odors.

It is essential to conduct a patch test before using it. Other methods include:

If you want to reduce inflammation and speed up the healing process, soak a clean cloth in fresh urine, and then apply it to the damaged area. Acne, eczema, and psoriasis are some of the most common skin conditions that can be treated using this method.

A excellent technique to relax and get sore muscles to feel better is to take a warm bath with some urine added to it. Urine's antibacterial properties might make it more effective in warding off disease and accelerating the healing process after illness.

Urine as a hair rinse has been demonstrated to improve the condition of the scalp and hair, as well as stimulate the growth of new hair on the scalp and in the hair itself. Urine has a potent odor; because of this, it is recommended that it be diluted with water before being applied to the hair.

Foot smell, fungal infections, and dry, cracked skin can all be alleviated by soaking the feet in a solution made of urine and warm water.

If you urinate into a cotton ball and then dab your face with it afterward, you can use your urine as a facial toner. Urine's natural exfoliating properties can assist in the elimination of acne by sloughing off dead skin cells that accumulate on the surface of the skin.

Urine can be used as an efficient mouthwash and gargled for the treatment of sore throats as well as the prevention of oral and throat infections. After using the gargle, you should spit the urine out and then thoroughly rinse your mouth with water.

It has been demonstrated that soaking your nails in a solution consisting of urine and warm water will both strengthen the nails and lower the likelihood of developing nail fungus.

You can try using some urine as eye drops to treat eye infections, which will also help reduce redness and irritation. You should only use fresh urine, and you should keep it away from your eyes.

Urine has been demonstrated to minimize the risk of infection and hasten the healing of wounds when it is applied to wounds in the form of a bandage. Be cautious to give a wound a good cleaning first, and if it's a major cut, consult a medical professional before using urine to treat it.

Urine, combined with a carrier oil such as co-conut or almond oil, can be utilized to produce an all-natural massage oil that, when applied topically, results in increased blood flow and decreased inflammation.

BENEFITS OF EXTERNAL URINE THERAPY

Urine therapy, also known as external urine therapy or urethral therapy, is the practice of applying urine externally to various parts of the body, including the skin, hair, and nails, for medicinal purposes. This method, while some may consider to be unique, actually has strong roots in established medical paradigms and is quickly growing in popularity among the community of alternative health practitioners. In the next section, we will investigate the practice of external urine therapy and the various ways in which it may assist individuals in leading better lives.

Skin Treatment

Since time immemorial, urethral therapy, also known as external urine therapy, has been utilized in the treatment of various skin disorders. When applied topically, urine has the potential to provide a number of benefits to the skin, including the following:

A gentle exfoliant, urine contains urea, which can be found in urine. When applied topically, urine has the capacity to both exfoliate the skin and encourage the creation of new skin cells, both of which are helpful to the general appearance of the skin as well as its health.

Moisturizers are still another alternative to consider. Urine contains the humectant known as urea. Urine also contains water. The usage of humectants is necessary in order to prevent the skin from becoming dehydrated. Urine, when applied topically to the skin, has the capacity to hydrate and moisturize the skin, which can be especially beneficial for persons who have dry skin or skin that is dehydrated.

Additionally, it may be useful in the treatment of acne. Because urine contains naturally occurring antibacterial and anti-fungal properties, acne can be avoided and germs can be eradicated using this natural remedy. If used topically, urine's anti-inflammatory and anti-redness qualities can aid in the treatment of acne and help prevent further outbreaks.

There are a number of nutrients in urine that are good for the skin, including amino acids. Urine has been shown to provide anti-aging effects when applied topically, including increased skin elasticity and a diminished appearance of fine lines and wrinkles. The antibacterial properties of urine can be used to combat skin illnesses by killing off microorganisms. People who suffer from skin disorders like eczema or psoriasis may benefit greatly from this.

Skin disorders like eczema and psoriasis can be helped by the antibacterial and anti-inflammatory qualities found in urine. Urine has anti-inflammatory and antimicrobial properties that can help alleviate skin problem symptoms when applied topically. Finally, athlete's foot and toenail fungus can be treated with urine because of its anti-fungal properties. Urine has anti-fungal and antibacterial properties, making it an effective topical treatment for fungal infections.

Hair Treatment

One of the most notable advantages of using external urine therapy is the possibility that it will promote the growth of good hair and a healthy scalp. In this chapter, we are going to discuss the many different ways in which external urine therapy may be beneficial to your hair.

Aids Hair Development. Urine is a great supply of minerals and nutrients, including potassium, calcium, and magnesium, all of which contribute to strong hair. Urine is also an excellent source of phosphorus, which is essential for healthy skin and nails. When applied topically to the scalp and hair, urine has been demonstrated to reverse hair loss, increase hair growth, and nourish hair follicles, all of which are necessary for healthy hair. In addition, the amino acids and other nutrients that are present in urine contribute to the overall health of the hair.

Adds Sheen and Enhances Texture to Hair. Urea, which is abundant in urine, functions as a natural exfoliator, assisting in the removal of dry, flaky skin cells from the scalp and hair. Urine has been shown to enhance hair texture and shine by eliminating debris from the scalp. Hair that is softer and shines more thanks to the alkaline pH of urine can also assist restore the scalp's natural pH balance.

The antibacterial properties of urine are capable of eliminating the bacteria and fungi that are the root of dandruff and other conditions that affect the scalp. You may prevent these issues from occurring on your scalp and promote its overall health by using urine in a topical application.

It will also restore the natural color of your hair, which is still another advantage. The yellow color that is distinctive of urine is caused by a pigment called urochrome. When applied topically to the hair, urochrome has the potential to assist in the highlighting process as well as the restoration of the natural color of the hair.

Deodorises Hair. Urine naturally contains urea, an ingredient that has natural deodorizing properties and can help cover unpleasant odors in the hair. Utilizing urine as a topical application is a great way to eliminate undesirable odors and leave hair smelling clean and revitalized.

Natural and Cost-Effective Hair Treatment. In case you were wondering, yes, urine may be used as a cheap and natural hair treatment that will help keep your scalp and hair in good condition. If you want to boost your hair's health without spending a fortune on store-bought treatments, urine is a cheap and easily accessible alternative.

- **Emotional Benefits**

The act of massaging urine into one's skin, hair, or nails has been found to be a very soothing and peaceful experience by a significant number of people. Self-care, often known as giving oneself time and attention, can be an effective method for achieving peace and unwinding one's mind and body. Urine contains urea, which has been shown to have a relaxing and stress-busting effect on the body, in addition to having a moisturizing effect on the skin.

A greater sense of self-worth and confidence are gained. The utilization of external urine therapy may result in an individual experiencing a boost in their feelings of self-worth as well as their level of self-assurance. A significant number of individuals assert that they were able to achieve greater levels of confidence after applying urine topically to their skin, hair, or nails. This could be due to the fact that individuals associate the activity with positive outcomes, such as healthier skin or stronger nails, or it could be due to the fact that it represents an opportunity to practice self-care and put one's own well-being at the forefront of one's priorities.

External Urine Improves Mood and Well-Being. Positive effects on one's disposition and sense of well-being may also result from external urine therapy. Self-love and the practice of self-care have been shown to have positive effects on one's emotional state. Using urine topically has also been linked to an increased sense of well-being because of the reported connection some people report having to their body and their health.

A Biological Strategy for Mental Health. The use of external urine therapy is a non-invasive method of improving mental health. Urine therapy makes use of a material that is naturally produced by the body, as opposed to pharmaceuticals or other interventions. This all-natural method may appeal to some people more than interventions that use man-made chemicals.

Awareness of the body and its demands may also improve with the help of external urine therapy. It has been suggested that including urine into one's self-care routine can help raise awareness of one's physical and mental wellbeing. A person's health and well-being can benefit from their greater awareness of any problems or areas where improvement is possible.

- **Wound-Healing Benefits**

In order for a wound to heal properly, it is necessary for a variety of cellular, tissue, and biochemical components to cooperate with one another. External urine therapy is a practice that has been practiced for millennia as a natural remedy, and recent scientific tests have shown that it is effective in promoting wound healing.

The bioactive molecules in urine, such as growth factors, cytokines, and antibacterial agents, can be beneficial to wounds if they are applied topically. Urine used topically to wounds possesses antibacterial, anti-inflammatory, and wound-healing qualities and can speed the healing process.

Urine contains an important component known as urea, which promotes the healing of wounds. Urea is a natural exfoliant that can be used to get rid of dead skin and speed up the natural regeneration process of the skin. It does this by loosening the bonds that hold dead skin cells together. Because of its antibacterial and proliferative qualities, urea is an excellent candidate for application topically in the process of wound debridement. As a consequence of this, the wound might heal more rapidly and there might be a lower risk of infection.

Urine contains a variety of growth factors that accelerate the repair and recovery of damaged tissues and wounds. One such protein is called epidermal growth factor (EGF), and it has been shown to hasten the healing of wounds by promoting the development and division of cells. TGF-beta, also known as transforming growth factor-beta, is a protein that has been shown to speed up the healing process in animal studies and also has similar effects on the regulation of cell proliferation.

Urine possesses antibacterial characteristics that aid in wound infection prevention and also promote tissue regeneration. The antibacterial urea, uric acid, and creatinine found in urine can assist to kill bacteria and stop the growth of fungus and other pathogens. This is especially crucial for open or polluted wounds, both of which increase the risk of infection.

When used properly, external urine therapy can be a healthy and efficient method of accelerating the healing of wounds. However, it's important to practice good hygiene and talk to a doctor before applying urine topically to wounds. Urine therapy may also not be appropriate for people who have specific allergies or health issues. In the right hands, external urine therapy has been shown to hasten wound healing and boost general health and wellness.

9
URINE THERAPY FOR SKIN CONDITIONS

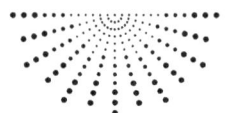

$\mathcal{I}$n the previous chapter, we briefly discussed the benefits of external urine therapy and its potential as a natural remedy for wound healing. But in this chapter, we shall explore the topic of urine therapy for skin diseases in greater detail. Urine therapy can help relieve symptoms and speed healing from a variety of skin disorders, including rashes, infections, and irritations.

To begin, know that the idea of using urine to treat skin issues is not novel. In fact, it's been around for centuries and used by a wide variety of cultures. Urea, amino acids, and minerals can all be found in urine and may prove useful in the treatment of skin disorders.

Urine therapy is used to treat a variety of skin problems, including eczema, which is extremely common. Patches of dry, itchy, and inflamed skin are the hallmark of the chronic skin disorder known as eczema. Urine therapy may be useful for symptom relief due to its ability to hydrate the skin and decrease inflammation. Using a cotton swab or other soft material, apply fresh urine to the eczema-affected area. Don't rinse off the urine just yet; let it a few minutes to work. If you want to see progress in your symptoms, you'll need to do this multiple times a day.

Acne, a common skin ailment caused by clogged hair follicles and bacterial overgrowth, can also be effectively treated with urine therapy. Urine's natural antibacterial capabilities can help eliminate bacteria and stop further outbreaks. Acne can be treated with urine treatment by dabbing a cotton ball or soft cloth with fresh urine and applying it to the afflicted region. Don't rinse off the urine just yet; let it a few minutes to work. If you want to see an improvement in your symptoms, you need to do this every day.

Psoriasis, a persistent autoimmune ailment that leads to the buildup of skin cells, is another skin problem that can be helped by urine therapy. Urine's anti-inflammatory and anti-drying characteristics make it a useful remedy for dry, itchy skin. Applying fresh urine to the afflicted area with a cotton ball or soft cloth is all that is required to perform urine treatment for psoriasis. Don't rinse off the urine just yet; let it a few minutes to work. If you want to see progress in your symptoms, you'll need to do this multiple times a day.

Urine therapy, while potentially helpful as a natural solution for skin issues, should not be considered a replacement for conventional medical care. A doctor should be consulted if you have a serious skin disease or if your symptoms persist despite treatment with urine. When treating skin conditions with urine therapy, it's also important to maintain a high standard of personal hygiene.

Several skin conditions may respond well to eternal urine therapy. If you use urine for its healing properties, you may be able to reduce discomfort and see recovery without resorting to artificial substances. Urine therapy, when used properly, has the potential to be a safe and successful method for enhancing one's skin health and general well-being.

URINE THERAPY TO TREAT SKIN CONDITIONS

Urine Therapy For Acne

The fact that urine therapy for acne is completely self-generated makes its naturalness one of the most appealing characteristics of this treatment method. Urine therapy has been shown to be effective in treating acne. It has been hypothesized that the antibacterial and anti-fungal compounds that are present in urine are capable of effectively treating acne that ranges from moderate to severe. Urotherapy, which refers to the practice of using one's own urine for medicinal purposes, is an option that is not only affordable but also readily available to everybody.

Urine therapy is considered to be one of the more natural treatments for acne; nevertheless, it is not necessarily the most comfortable choice. According to research conducted in laboratories, more than ninety percent of urine is composed of water. The remaining ten percent consists of urea, ammonia, salt, and various minerals, some of which have been associated with healing powers and a reduction in acne. Because it is an antibacterial and anti-fungal agent that is particularly effective, urea is frequently utilized in the treatment of skin conditions such as psoriasis and eczema. This will be discussed in further detail later on in this chapter. This is believed to hydrate the skin, protecting it from the drying effects of chemical acne treatments. This is in addition to the urine salt, which helps in the retention of moisture.

It is a widely held misconception that urine is "dirty" and teeming with microorganisms and bacteria. However, recent scientific study has demonstrated that, in reality, urine is "sterile" and free of germs; in fact, it is even considered cleaner than distilled water. This contradicts the conventional belief that urine is unclean. Not only is it free of any infectious agents, but it also contains minute quantities of a wide range of vitamins and minerals. Urine is a fluid that is produced by filtering blood and contains waste items that have been carried across the body by the circulatory system. For instance, if a person takes in an excessive amount of vitamin C, the kidney will expel it from the body through urine if there is too much of it in the system. Because urine contains vitamins and minerals like vitamins B, C, iron, and zinc, in addition to amino acids like tryptophan, lysine, and methionine, there is a possibility that urine therapy for acne could be beneficial.

Urine therapy for acne is also very cost-effective. This is due to the fact that the individual getting treatment does not need to buy very much urine, and urine is not difficult to acquire. On the other hand, one can find that in order to produce more "nutritious" urine, they need to spend money on particular foods and beverages. Fruits and vegetables, as well as cranberry juice and apple cider vinegar, are some examples of foods that fall into this category. Because "morning urine," also known as the first fluid that is excreted after waking up, contains the highest concentration of vitamins and urea, practitioners of alternative medicine recommend drinking it. Morning urine is the first fluid that is expelled in the morning. Orally or topically applying urine as a treatment for acne are the two possible routes of administration. The latter option, on the other hand, is generally preferred and may result in larger advantages due to the direct absorption that occurs via the skin.

Urine Therapy For Eczema

Eczema is a common skin condition that, in certain cases, can be helped by applying urine topically. Eczema, also known as atopic dermatitis, is a chronic inflammatory skin illness that is characterized by itchy, dry areas of skin that are accompanied by inflammation. It is possible for this condition to be caused by a combination of environmental and genetic factors, such as coming into touch with irritants or allergens.

By applying fresh urine to the skin that is affected by eczema, the aim of urine therapy for eczema is to alleviate irritation and accelerate the healing process. Urine contains urea, amino acids, and minerals, all of which have been demonstrated to have a soothing and moisturizing impact on the skin. Urine also reduces inflammation. Urea has been shown to be particularly effective in lowering the symptoms of eczema. It does this by increasing the synthesis of new skin cells while also eliminating the old ones.

When applied to skin that has just been bathed, the urine therapy for eczema is at its most effective. To clean the area, first use a moderate amount of soap and warm water, and then pat it dry with care thereafter. Using a cotton ball or a gentle towel, the following step is to dab the affected region with freshly urinated urine. Wait a few minutes before rinsing off the urine so that it has time to do its job. You will need to perform this action numerous times per day in order to observe any improvement in your symptoms.

It should be noted, however, that not all urine is created equal when it comes to the treatment of eczema using urine. Urinating first thing in the morning is typically preferred by individuals because the urine produced at this time of day is perceived to be more concentrated and to include a greater quantity of beneficial substances, such as urea. Because urine that has been sitting around for a while may contain bacteria and other potentially harmful components, it is essential to always use fresh urine.

Urine therapy for eczema is not intended to be used in place of standard medical treatment despite the possibility that it may be beneficial. If your symptoms are severe or continue for an extended period of time, it is advised that you seek medical attention. When using urine therapy to treat eczema, it is essential to maintain a clean environment. Make sure that your hands are clean both before and after using any product by giving them a good scrub with soap and water.

Urine therapy has demonstrated a great deal of potential as a non-pharmaceutical treatment option for eczema. Urine includes a number of beneficial elements that can be applied to the treatment of a variety of conditions and the acceleration of the healing process without the use of potentially dangerous chemicals or pharmaceuticals. Urine therapy has the potential to be a risk-free and effective way for improving both the health of one's skin and their overall well-being when it is used in the correct manner.

Urine Therapy For Psoriasis

Psoriasis is a chronic autoimmune disorder that causes skin cells to build up, resulting in scales and red patches on the affected area. This illness, which can lead to significant levels of discomfort and anguish, affects around 125 million people all over the world. Psoriasis can be treated using a variety of approaches, including lotions that are rubbed into the affected area of skin, medications that are taken orally, or even light treatment.

Urine treatment, on the other hand, has recently come to the forefront as a competitive option.

Psoriasis can be treated by applying fresh urine directly to the affected areas of the skin. Urine, despite the fact that some people may find the idea of utilizing it as a cure to be repulsive or even unclean, does contain a number of beneficial compounds that can be utilized in the treatment of psoriasis.

Urine is an excellent source of urea, which can be used as a treatment for psoriasis. Urea is a natural moisturizer that can be used to help soften and moisturize dry, flaky skin by applying it to the affected areas. Psoriasis sufferers, who frequently have thick, scaly patches of skin, will especially like the fact that its exfoliating abilities can be excellent for eliminating dead skin cells. This is because psoriasis sufferers typically have thick, scaly patches of skin.

The mineral content of urine, which includes potassium and magnesium, as well as a number of other elements, is responsible for its anti-inflammatory and skin-soothing qualities. The immune cells and antibodies that can be present in urine have the potential to reduce the immunological response caused by psoriasis.

If you wish to use your urine as a treatment for your psoriasis, you must first make certain that the urine is clean. It is possible to achieve this goal by collecting the urine in the middle of the stream after the vaginal region has been meticulously cleaned. It is possible to apply the urine to the skin in issue by dabbing it on with a cotton ball or a gentle cloth. Urine contains beneficial components that can be absorbed by the skin, however this process requires that the urine be left on the skin for at least a few minutes.

Even though urine therapy has shown some patients suffering from psoriasis that it may be helpful, this treatment should not be considered a replacement for standard medical care. Patients with severe cases of psoriasis or those whose symptoms do not improve despite treatment with urine should consult a medical professional. When treating psoriasis with urine therapy, it is essential to practice proper hygiene at all times. To prevent contamination, you should always use fresh urine and wash your hands thoroughly before and after applying the solution.

Patients who suffer from psoriasis may find that urine therapy provides them with relief from their symptoms and improves the overall health of their skin. Psoriasis sufferers who use their own urine as a cure for the condition, which may sound unusual at first, can get relief from the symptoms of the condition. Like any other alternative treatment for psoriasis, urine therapy for psoriasis should first be discussed with a medical professional, and good hygiene should be observed throughout the administration process.

TIPS FOR EFFECTIVE TREATMENT OF SKIN CONDITIONS WITH URINE THERAPY

Natural remedies like urine treatment have been used for ages to treat skin diseases like eczema, acne, psoriasis, and others. However, there are certain recommendations and rules to follow in order to maximize the efficacy of urine therapy. Some helpful hints for using urine therapy to treat skin disorders are presented here.

Use only fresh urinate: Fresh urine has the largest concentration of active chemicals, making it the most effective for external therapy. Urine that has been laying about for an extended period of time may have bacteria that are dangerous to your health.

Before applying urine to the skin, wash the area with mild soap and water to remove any dirt or debris. This will stop the discomfort and infection in its tracks.

To treat an injury, urinate on it. Use a cotton ball or a delicate cloth to dab some urine onto the injured region. If you want the urine to have the most effect, you need to put it on the damaged area directly.

The urine should be left on the skin for a few minutes after application, and then washed off with warm water. This will increase the urine's effectiveness by facilitating the absorption of its active ingredients through the skin.

For optimal outcomes, the urine therapy treatment should be repeated multiple times daily. This will aid in providing consistent symptom alleviation and speeding up the healing process.

It's crucial to keep an eye on the skin when it's being treated. It may be necessary to seek medical attention if symptoms intensify or continue.

If you want your urine therapy to be as effective as possible, it's important to stay hydrated and drink enough of water.

It's crucial to be patient and consistent with urine therapy because it may take some time to see improvements.Aloe vera, coconut oil, and tea tree oil are just a few examples of other natural therapies that can be used in conjunction with urine therapy to increase its effectiveness and bring even more relief.

Get in Touch with Your Doctor: If symptoms persist or worsen, it is best to see a doctor to rule out more serious problems and discuss treatment options.

As we have shown, urine therapy is a viable natural option for treating a number of skin disorders. If you want to get the most out of urine therapy for external use, it's important to follow these rules. Always use clean urine and keep an eye on your skin when receiving therapy. Urine therapy can help relieve symptoms and improve skin health if used regularly and with patience.

URINE THERAPY FOR DIGESTIVE HEALTH

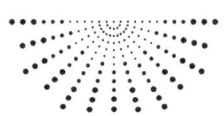

*U*rotherapy, often known as urine therapy, refers to the use of urine for therapeutic purposes. Although the use of urine as a means of treatment may sound strange at first, it has actually been practiced for millennia as part of the conventional medical system in some societies. Urine therapy has been argued to improve intestinal health and provide other benefits by its proponents. However, it should be noted that this therapy is not widely approved or endorsed by the medical profession, and questions remain about its efficacy and safety.

The kidneys secrete urine as a waste product to flush the system of poisons and excess chemicals.

Mostly water and urea with some electrolytes and trace quantities of other chemicals. Some people believe that urine therapy can help with digestive health because of the vitamins, minerals, enzymes, and hormones that are purported to be present in urine.

Urine therapy for digestive health issues is advocated in part because of the possible antibacterial characteristics of urine. Some people believe that the antibacterial and antiviral properties of urine can help fight against infections in the digestive tract. Urine contains waste materials and is that the body is seeking to expel; hence, its use as a therapeutic agent may have undesirable side effects.

Urine therapy has the potential to increase digestion and promote gut health, which is another advantage commonly cited for it. Some people believe that enzymes in urine, like amylase and protease, can aid in the digestion of carbohydrates and proteins. While it's true that the digestive system develops its own enzymes to aid in digestion, there is a lack of supporting scientific proof for these assertions.

It's important to remember that medical professionals don't recommend using urine treatment for anything, including gastrointestinal health. Before starting urine therapy, you should learn about the possible risks and adverse effects. The bacteria, viruses, and toxins found in urine vary from person to person based on factors like nutrition, lifestyle, and medication use. A person who drinks their own urine may be exposing themselves to harmful microorganisms and toxins.

USING URINE THERAPY TO IMPROVE DIGESTIVE HEALTH

An ancient technique has just emerged from the depths of history to grab the imagination of a few of committed individuals who are looking for alternative approaches to health and wellness. Urine therapy is a fascinating method that has been connected to significant enhancements in digestive health and wellness. Despite the fact that some people might find the idea to be bizarre or even ludicrous, those who support it are adamant in their claim that it has some sort of worth.

Urine, a byproduct of human physiology that is typically ignored, is the focus of this novel and novelly innovative project. urine is made up largely of water, urea, electrolytes, and trace components; however, proponents of urine therapy argue that it also contains a variety of therapeutic properties, such as vitamins, minerals, enzymes, and even hormones that can be beneficial to our weaker digestive systems. urine is collected from the urinary tract and stored in the kidneys until it is expelled from the body.

The antibacterial properties of urine are frequently stated as the primary reason why it is advised as a treatment for gastrointestinal illnesses. Urine has been shown to be effective in treating gastrointestinal disorders. It has been suggested that urine, due to the presence of natural antibodies and antibacterial chemicals in its composition, could be an efficient weapon against pathogenic bacteria found in the digestive tract.

In addition, adherents of this esoteric practice extol its virtues for enhancing digestive function and fostering healthy gastrointestinal tracts. It is believed that the body stores a lot of digestive enzymes, including amylase and protease, which are responsible for breaking down carbohydrates and proteins, in the urine. Regrettably, there is a dearth of evidence to back up these assertions. Since the human body is capable of producing its own digestive enzymes, it is possible that taking enzyme supplements that are found in urine is not required.

Although urine therapy has a number of ardent proponents, it is essential to be aware of the considerable skepticism that exists among the medical community. There is just a little amount of consensus that treating digestive issues or any other ailment with urine therapy is an efficient strategy to improve overall health. Urine, depending on the state of a person's health, the foods they eat, and the medications they take, may contain germs, viruses, and toxins; as a result, the risks and adverse effects of using this method should not be disregarded.

TREATING GASTRITIS, CONSTIPATION, AND DIARRHEA WITH URINE THERAPY

Urine therapy is an intriguing practice that may be traced back to ancient civilizations. It has lately come to the attention of the public as a result of claims that it can treat a range of gastrointestinal conditions. Gastritis, constipation, and diarrhea are all conditions that cause discomfort and make it difficult to go about one's everyday life; as a result, one should not discount the chance that an alternative treatment would acquire popularity.

Gastritis

The stomach lining can become inflamed, irritated, or eroded for a variety of reasons, which is known as gastritis. Gastritis is not just one disease, but a condition with several potential origins. Pain or discomfort in the upper part of the abdomen is a common symptom of gastritis regardless of its source. This condition is also known as dyspepsia.

Chronic gastritis is characterized by long-lasting symptoms like loss of appetite or nausea, while acute gastritis is characterized by short-term, severe symptoms lasting a day or two, depending on the origin of the inflammation.

The symptoms of the rarer types of gastritis can be far more severe, though. Inflammation is rarely a symptom of erosive gastritis, but the condition can progress to serious complications like internal bleeding or stomach ulcers. Rarely, the helicobacter pylori (H. pylori) bacteria can cause gastritis known as chronic atrophic gastritis, which is characterized by the atrophy of cells in the stomach lining and the destruction of the mucosal barrier that protects the stomach. This can increase the risk of developing stomach cancer. Chronic, atrophic gastritis has been linked to the gastrointestinal illness pernicious anemia.

Symptoms of Gastritis

- Acute and chronic gastritis typically cause the following symptoms, though in some circumstances the condition may be asymptomatic:
- The loss of appetite is a common sign of chronic gastritis.
- Loss of appetite and nausea are common symptoms of nausea.
- Indigestion, often known as dyspepsia, causes discomfort or pain in the upper belly. After eating, the pain may occur or become more severe.
- Nausea and vomiting are symptoms of all types of gastritis. If there is blood in the vomit, it could mean that the stomach lining has been damaged and ulcers have

formed. The color of the vomit varies from crimson to the appearance of coffee grounds, depending on the degree of ulceration.

- Melaena refers to bloody diarrhea. The blood turns the feces a dark color, almost black or tarry.

Urine Therapy Treatment Conditions For Gastritis

Envision yourself enjoying a cappuccino at a local cafe when you overhear a couple at the next table exchanging heated words about an alternative treatment for gastritis. Their topic of choice? Urine therapy. Now, before you cringe or spill your coffee, let's dive into the medical aspects of this debate.

For the uninitiated, gastritis is an inflammation of the lining of the stomach that can lead to pain, discomfort, and other digestive problems. It's not surprising that people who are suffering from this condition want to try anything to get better. This is where the concept of urine therapy comes into play.

Supporters of urine therapy are convinced that the human body's own "liquid gold" might be an effective tool in the fight against gastritis. It does sound odd at first, but please hear me out. Some people believe that the unique properties found in urine can help reduce inflammation and associated uncomfortable effects. They suggest that the antibodies and antibacterial compounds found in urine can fight the germs that cause gastrointestinal irritation.

Urine therapy for gastritis is a good example of the kind of alternative medicine that can elicit passionate discussion. It's a sobering reminder that in the complex realm of medical research, competing theories and philosophies can make for confusing reading.

Here, however, is a hypothetical step-by-step approach that some advocates of urine therapy may advise for treating gastritis:

- Step 1: Ensure hygiene and collection:

Advocates of urine therapy stress the significance of hygienic collection practices. They may suggest disinfecting the collection container, ensuring the urine is fresh, and cleaning hands properly before collecting it.

- Step 2: Start with small amounts:

Some advocates of using urine as a treatment for gastritis recommend starting with a very low dose. Taking a few drops diluted in water or adding it to other drinks or herbal teas are all viable options.

- Step 3: Raise Consumption Moderately

Advocates of urine therapy have proposed that patients gradually increase their urine intake. Although different advocates may advocate for somewhat different steps, most agree that the dosage should be gradually increased while being closely monitored to account for the body's reaction.

- Step 4: Keep an eye on any adverse effects:

Keep a close eye on your gastritis symptoms and general health when you undergo urine therapy treatment. Keep track of your progress and any side effects you experience so you may share this information with your provider.

- Step 5: Integrate with a healthy lifestyle:

Many who support urine therapy also stress the need for a change to a healthier lifestyle. Eating well, controlling stress, maintaining a regular exercise routine, and employing other forms of self-care can all contribute to better digestive health.

- Step 6: Regular check-ups:

It is important to keep up with your regular checkups with your healthcare practitioner regardless of whether you decide to pursue urine therapy or another alternative treatment. They will be able to keep an eye on your health, offer advice, and make sure you get the care you need.

Constipation

There are a few main signs that describe constipation. Passing less than three stools per week, passing stools that are difficult to pass, hard or dry, including blood, causing severe rectal or abdominal pain, and a feeling that a stool has not been entirely passed are all signs that should be taken seriously. In most cases, medical care is unnecessary when only mild symptoms are present. However, if you experience serious symptoms like blood in your stools or need to physically remove feces, you should visit a doctor.

Causes & Risks Factors

Too little movement of feces through the digestive tract is the most common cause of constipation. Stools that move too slowly are less likely to be passed, which increases the risk of constipation and dryness. There are many potential causes of a sluggish bowel movement. Constipation can be caused by a number of conditions, including cancer, intestinal obstruction, bowel strictures, and anal fissures. Additionally, neurological disorders can impact nerves that aid in the digestive process by facilitating the movement of feces. Spinal cord injuries, multiple sclerosis, and Parkinson's disease are all examples of such conditions. Muscular issues are a possible underlying reason as well. Stool dysfunction can be caused by weak pelvic muscles, dyssynergia in the pelvic muscles, or anismus (the inability to relax the pelvic muscles). Sometimes hormones are involved as well. Pregnancy, diabetes, and an under-active thyroid have all been linked to disruptions in fluid-regulating hormones.

Constipation can be caused by a number different things. Women and the elderly are more prone to constipation. Mental health illnesses such as depression and eating disorders, as well as dehydration, a low-fiber diet, a sedentary lifestyle, certain drugs, and more, all increase the risk.

Urine Therapy Treatment Conditions For Constipation

Let's delve even further into the issue of constipation and investigate how urine therapy is said to alleviate the condition.

Constipation is a common problem that can cause discomfort and frustration for those who suffer from it. The same symptoms of discomfort, bloating, and straining that I've been describing recently appear when bowel motions become sporadic or difficult. Although there are many options for dealing with constipation, some advocates of alternative medicines believe that urine therapy could be the answer.

Some people claim that drinking urine can help with constipation since it stimulates the digestive tract and can lead to more frequent bowel movements. Urine contains enzymes including amylase and protease, which they say help break down carbs and proteins. If this theory is correct, then consuming urine could help those who suffer from constipation by increasing the amount of digestive enzymes entering the system.

- Understanding Urine Therapy:

Learn about urine treatment and its alleged benefits in treating constipation. Make sure you have a deep understanding of the subject by doing research and consulting credible sources.

- Safety and hygiene

Keep up with standard procedures for cleanliness and safety at all times. Make sure the containers you use to collect and store urine are clean and sterile, and always wash your hands before and after handling urine.

- Collection:

Urine should be collected in a sterile container. The "morning urine," the first urine of the day, is frequently regarded as the most effective for medicinal purposes. Avoid cross-contamination by using a container with a wide mouth.

- Storage:

Urine should be kept in a dark, cool environment to inhibit the growth of microorganisms. Some advocates recommend storing the product in a glass jar with a secure lid. Keep the container away from anything edible or drinkable, and label it clearly.

- Dilution:

Many people who advocate for the consumption of urine advise first diluting it with water. Generally, it is recommended to dilute urine with water at a ratio of one part urine to multiple parts water. The therapeutic components should remain but the concentration of potentially hazardous compounds should be reduced.

- Gradual Introduction:

You should begin with drinking only a little amount of diluted urine and work up to larger volumes later. Many advocates stress the need of starting with a modest dose and gradually increasing it over time. By easing into it, your body has time to acclimate and less negative effects are experienced.

- Timing and Frequency:

Some advocates of urine therapy recommend taking it first thing in the morning on an empty stomach. However, people's tastes can vary greatly. You can try out various intervals and repetition rates to see what works best for you. Always pay attention to how your body reacts and stop if necessary.

- Monitoring and Adjustment:

Keep track of your progress as you use urine treatment. Keep an eye on your bowel motions, how you're feeling, and how you're doing generally. If you experience any negative reactions or a worsening of symptoms, you should stop the treatment and see a doctor very once.

Diarrhea

Diarrhea is characterized by bowel movements that are more loose, watery, or frequent than usual.

It's common, and most people experience it occasionally, but it's usually not anything to worry about. It's not nice and may even cause you distress. In most cases, the condition improves within a week.

Causes

Diarrhea can result from a wide variety of factors. The most prevalent cause, in both infants and adults, is an infection of the digestive tract (gastroenteritis).

Causes of gastroenteritis include:

- one or more viruses, like noroviruses or rotaviruses
- campylobacter and other pathogenic bacteria
- Food-borne Escherichia coli (E. coli) infections are common.
- a parasite, like the one that causes

giardiasis and can be found in polluted water systems

It is possible to contract such diseases when overseas, especially in locations with inadequate sanitation services. Traveller's diarrhea is the name for this condition.

Urine Therapy Treatment Conditions For Diarrhea

Infections, food poisoning, pharmaceutical side effects, and underlying medical disorders are only few of the many potential causes of diarrhea, characterized by frequent loose or watery stools. Proponents of urine therapy claim that it can help with diarrhea management.

Diarrhea may subside in part because urine includes chemicals that help the body rebalance its salts and fluids. They claim that electrolytes like sodium, potassium, and chloride can be found in urine and are essential for staying hydrated and having a healthy electrolyte balance.

Step 1: Collecting urine

Urine collection is the initial step in treating diarrhea using urine. Urine should be collected after the initial flow has stopped, in the midstream, for optimal utilization. It's also crucial to use a sanitary collection method for the urine.

Step 2: Diluting urine

Before drinking, dilute the collected urine with clean water. It is suggested that one part urine be mixed with two to three parts water.

Step 3: Consuming urine

Urine is diluted and then taken orally. One tablespoon is a good starting point, and the dose can be increased from there.

Step 4: Repeating the process

Collecting, diluting, and ingesting urine on a daily basis is necessary to reap the therapeutic benefits of urine therapy for diarrhea.

BEST PRACTICES FOR INCORPORATING URINE THERAPY INTO A DIGESTIVE HEALTH REGIMEN

Adding urine therapy to your routine for digestive health should be done with caution because it is a controversial alternative medicine. In terms of digestive health, there is a dearth of research demonstrating the efficacy and safety of urine therapy. It's important to talk to a experienced professional before trying any alternative remedies.

Here are some pointers for anyone interested in further investigating urine treatment for gastrointestinal wellness:

Before adding urine therapy to your routine for digestive health, it is important to speak with a skilled healthcare expert. They are in the best position to advise you, assess your illness, and give you all the information you need to choose the best course of therapy.

If you decide to undertake urine therapy, it is imperative that you observe strict standards of cleanliness and safety. Collect urine in clean containers and always wash your hands before and after working with urine. Many urine therapy advocates stress the importance of diluting urine with water before ingesting it. The standard recommendation is to mix one part urine with two or three parts water. Some chemicals that may be present in urine may be attenuated by diluting the urine.

If you choose to try drinking urine that has been diluted, start with a little amount, like a table-spoon, and build up to larger amounts only if you feel safe doing so. Pay attention to how your body reacts, and stop using it if you get sick. Keep an eye on your general health while introducing alternative treatments like urine therapy into your current routine for digestive health. Document any shifts in your symptoms, bowel habits, or general health. Discontinue treatment and see a doctor immediately if you have any adverse reactions or a worsening of your disease.

It is important to prioritize evidence-based methods to digestive health while also considering alternative treatments. Maintain a healthy lifestyle by eating right, drinking enough of water, working out frequently, and controlling stress. There is a large body of evidence demonstrating the positive effects of these habits on digestive health.

Finally, keep in mind that the cornerstone of any digestive health program should be getting counsel from healthcare specialists and relying on evidence-based procedures. They'll listen to your individual concerns and offer recommendations for care based on the best available science.

11

URINE THERAPY FOR
IMMUNE SYSTEM SUPPORT

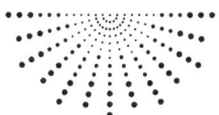

$\mathcal{I}$n the early nineteenth century, a physician by the name of Charles Ducan conducted research on the possible therapeutic value of self-produced substances such as urine. He demonstrated that patients with gonorrheal urethritis, which is an infection of the urinary tube caused by gonorrhea, are able to treat themselves with their own discharge, which acts as a type of self-medication. In this particular instance, auto-therapy was implemented by activating the body's natural healing processes by placing a drop of the patient's discharge on the patient's tongue. This medication proved successful in eradicating gonorrhea regardless of how far along in the progression of the disease it was supplied when it was given.

According to the findings of Dr. William D. Linscott's research, auto-therapy helps to strengthen and stimulate the immune system, particularly the T-cells. After receiving urine therapy, the T-cell counts of a few patients who had been diagnosed with low T-cell counts previous to treatment showed significant recovery. This demonstrated the efficacy of Urine Therapy in improving immunity. Below are some other immune boosting benefits of urine therapy.

THE IMMUNE-BOOSTING BENEFITS OF URINE THERAPY

According to a news report from Dailymail.co.uk, In the quiet town of Kent, an extraordinary story unfolds, challenging the conventional notions of healing and wellness. At the center of this story is Kayleigh Oakley, a vibrant yoga teacher who embarked on a journey that would forever change her life.

From a tender age, Kayleigh faced the arduous battle of a low immune system, a burden that cast a shadow over her every step. The weight of constant tiredness and nagging muscle pain became her constant companions, and life seemed to lose its vibrant colors. But the universe wasn't done testing her resilience just yet.

As she reached the pivotal age of fifteen, another challenge emerged from the depths of her being. Hashimoto's disease, an autoimmune condition, took hold, rendering her thyroid under-active. This added yet another layer of complexity to her already fragile state.

But fate had even more hardships in store for Kayleigh. Two years later, the weight of chronic fatigue and fibromyalgia settled upon her weary shoulders. Every simple task became a nightmare, and the pain that enveloped her body seemed insurmountable. Amidst the chaos, her loving husband Tristan, a draftsman of unwavering support, stood by her side, his presence a beacon of hope in the darkest of times.

The battle against her low immune system waged on for years, leaving Kayleigh bed-bound for days after even the most mundane outings. Yet, in the midst of despair, a flicker of hope emerged. With a mix of curiosity and desperation, she turned to an unconventional path: urine therapy.

Every morning, as the sun kissed the horizon, Kayleigh began her ritual. With courage coursing through her veins, she sipped from the cup of possibility, embracing the unknown. Days turned into weeks, and a remarkable transformation began to unfurl.

It was as if the universe itself conspired to grant Kayleigh a renewed lease on life. The heavy fog of chronic fatigue began to dissipate, replaced by a newfound energy that surged through her veins. Her once-sluggish thyroid awakened, as if stirred from a deep slumber, radiating vitality. And most astonishingly, her once-fragile immune system stood tall, fortified by an unseen strength.

Kayleigh reveled in the miraculous shift that had taken hold. She boldly proclaimed that urine therapy had become her guiding light, a beacon of healing that defied the skepticism of the medical community. In her eyes, it had cured her severe fatigue, reignited her dormant thyroid, and breathed life into her weakened immune system.

As her story echoed through the town, whispers of both wonder and doubt filled the air. Skeptics questioned the lack of scientific backing, while others marveled at the resilience of the human spirit. Yet, in the heart of Kayleigh Oakley, there was an unwavering conviction that her path to healing had taken an extraordinary turn.

Her journey serves as a reminder that sometimes, when faced with insurmountable odds, we must venture into uncharted territories. In the realm of unconventional methods lies the potential for remarkable transformations. It is in these unexplored realms that the boundaries of healing and wellness expand, beckoning us to question, to challenge, and to embrace the unexpected.

And so, the tale of Kayleigh Oakley continues to captivate, leaving us to ponder the extraordinary possibilities that lie within the depths of our own journeys. For in the face of adversity, it is our willingness to embrace the unknown that allows us to discover the true extent of our strength and resilience.

HOW URINE THERAPY CAN HELP PREVENT ILLNESS AND DISEASE

It's evident that Urine Therapy can aid in strengthening the immune system, which is made up of a variety of different bodily structures—organs, cells, tissues, and proteins. These work together to carry out physiological processes that defend the body from dangerous substances like bacteria and viruses.

Our immune system has a fascinating protection mechanism buried deep within its intricate inner workings, and it activates when faced with a dangerous toxin. When a virus gets into contact with the immune system, it sets off a spectacular chain of events known as the immunological response. Antibodies are secreted by the immune system in large quantities during this stage of the immunological response. These antibodies specifically target and bind to antigens displayed by invading pathogens, neutralizing and killing them in the process.

Urine therapy emerges as a potential friend in this intricate game of defense, providing a means to fortify the body's immune system. The immune system can be strengthened by the use of urine treatment. The immune system is boosted through urine therapy, making the patient more resistant to illness and disease. You may find a urine treatment program here. Instead of seeing urine therapy as a miracle cure, it should be seen as an adjunctive method that boosts the immune system and aids in disease prevention. This is a very important consideration that needs to be addressed.

The immune system plays a crucial role in protecting our bodies from illness. It keeps out harmful chemicals, bacteria, and viruses, as well as cellular changes that could cause illness, so that our bodies can function normally. Organs, cells, and proteins all work together to maintain our health and vitality, making our bodies complex systems.

When our immune system is functioning well, we don't have to give it any thought because it takes care of us automatically and imperceptibly. It eliminates threats and maintains the body's delicate balance without our awareness. However, when our immune systems are impaired, either because they have been weakened or because they are having trouble fending off particularly aggressive germs, our vulnerability to sickness increases. When our immune system encounters a pathogen it has never encountered before, it raises the risk of infection because our defenses may not be ready to mount an effective response. Certain germs, particularly those that cause childhood illnesses like chickenpox, can cause sickness after only one encounter. However, our immune system has the remarkable capability to change and improve when it encounters new antigens and threats. This process generates memory cells, which provide long-term defense against infection.

Therefore, urine therapy can be seen as an efficient method that substantially aids the target of general health. It does so by bolstering the immune system with nutrients, which in turn boosts the body's natural defenses and improves our ability to deal with the many threats we face. While it's important to recognize the boundaries of urine therapy and seek out evidence-based approaches to disease prevention and treatment, exploring other avenues that leverage the immune system's power may yield substantial insights and, ultimately, better health results. Urine therapy has its limitations, but it's still important to look for other ways to prevent and treat illness that have more solid scientific backing.

Within the intricate tapestry of human existence, the immune system weaves a tale of resistance and safety. It protects us against the invisible threats that exist all around us. Let us, as we navigate the delicate balance between health and illness, be open to the possibilities offered by urine therapy and other methods that strengthen and improve our immune system. By doing so, we will be well on our way to a life that is not just healthier but also more vibrant.

BEST PRACTICES FOR INCORPORATING URINE THERAPY INTO AN IMMUNE SYSTEM SUPPORT REGIMEN

Careful and cautious consideration must be given when deciding whether or not to use urine treatment as part of a program designed to boost the immune system. While this may be helpful for some, it's always best to get the OK from a doctor before making any major adjustments to your regular healthcare routine. Best practices for using urine treatment as part of an immune system support program include the following:

- Seek Professional Guidance by an Experienced Urine Therapist:

It is essential to see an expert in this area before deciding to include urine therapy to your routine of immune system maintenance. There are several reasons why it's important to not talk to a doctor about your health who is familiar with your case. They will laugh at you, they are not trained or knowledgable in this area. They only know about medicine and surgery.

A qualified urine therapist or provider is best equipped to weigh the pros and cons of urine therapy because to their extensive training and experience in this area. They are in a position to provide you an unbiased opinion on whether or not urine therapy is a good idea given your specific health situation. Considerations include things like the patient's history, any allergies they may have, any drugs they may be taking, and any particular sensitivities they may have. In light of these considerations, your healthcare provider can advise you on whether or not urine treatment is appropriate for you.

In addition, experts can quickly and easily obtain the most recent findings and empirical data. They will have the most recent and correct information on the effects of urine therapy on the immune system and how it works. Helping you sort through potentially confusing or misleading data, they can lead you through the current body of knowledge.

In addition, an expert can provide you with guidance that is based on your individual situation. They will be able to assess how your current treatments and interventions may interact with urine therapy. In addition, they can ensure you have a safe and successful routine by advising you on the right urine therapy dosage, frequency, and length.

• Research and Educate Yourself:

Making educated decisions regarding whether or not to use urine treatment in a regimen designed to boost the immune system requires research and education. The science and data underlying urine therapy might be confusing, so it's crucial to obtain information from trustworthy sources. Remember Big Pharma doesn't want you to stop using medication as that taps into their business model of keeping us sick.

There have been several investigations into the advantages and disadvantages of using urine treatment. For instance, Tsiplakou, Tentor, and Tsakris conducted research on the antibacterial characteristics of urine and reported that it includes chemicals that can suppress the growth of certain bacteria and fungus in the Journal of Clinical and Aesthetic Dermatology. Based on these results, urine treatment may be useful in boosting the immune system's ability to fight off dangerous bacteria.

The role of urine peptides in regulating immune responses was also recently reviewed in Current Opinion in Allergy and Clinical Immunology. The review underlined the fact that urine contains bioactive peptides that can affect immune cell function and help regulate the immune system. This establishes a rationale for further research into the efficacy of urine treatment in enhancing the immune system.

The hazards of urine therapy should not be disregarded, even though additional study and proof are required. The need of testing urine for pollutants and pathogens before using it in therapy was highlighted in a study published in the Journal of Renal Nutrition. This emphasizes the significance of taking all necessary safety measures before beginning any form of urine therapy.

Individuals can make educated judgments about using urine therapy in their immune system support routine by performing in-depth study and comprehending the scientific data. The possible benefits and hazards of urine treatment need to be carefully weighed before any decisions are made.

Additionally, speaking with experts versed in urine therapy might provide additional direction and understanding. They can aid in making sense of medical studies and give individualized recommendations based on unique health profiles.

It's important to proceed with caution and a focus on evidence-based information when adding urine treatment to a regimen designed to enhance the immune system. Individuals can make well-informed judgments about the benefits and hazards of urine treatment in bolstering immune system function by staying informed and taking into account the existing information.

• Hygiene and Safety

Urine therapy poses a danger of bacterial contamination if not performed with proper hygiene and safety measures in place. Essential hygiene procedures include collecting urine in a sterile container, storing it properly, washing hands thoroughly, and sterilizing equipment. Urine treatment has shown promise, but more research is needed to determine its overall safety and effectiveness. To confidently decide whether or not to incorporate urine therapy into your routine, you should seek professional counsel and keep up with the latest scientific information.

- Start Slowly and Monitor Your Body's Response:

If you want to use urine treatment as part of your routine to boost your immune system, make sure to ease into it and pay close attention to how your body reacts. If you're unsure of how your body will react, start with a modest volume of urine and see how you feel. By taking it easy at first, you can see how your body reacts to the routine and decide if it's right for you.

Harvard Medical School researchers have found that keeping tight tabs on your body's reaction to any new intervention is essential to your health and safety. By gradually increasing the amount of urine you drink, you can help your body adjust to the new routine. You can gauge any possible reactions or side effects with this careful approach.

Pay close attention to your physical sensations as you go along. Keep an eye out for any emotional or mental shifts you could experience after eating urine. Keep an eye on your strength, digestion, skin, and general health. Urine therapy should be stopped promptly and medical advice sought if any adverse effects, including gastrointestinal issues or allergic responses, occur.

According to Harvard Medical School, listening to your body and making necessary adjustments is essential. This method is consistent with the tenets of personalized medicine, which emphasize taking into account how each patient responds to treatment. Because of these differences, it's impossible to generalize about what would be best for everyone's health. Careful observation of your own physiological response can help you determine whether or not urine therapy is appropriate for your needs.

• Regular Monitoring and Check-ups:

Even when using urine therapy as part of an immune system support routine, regular checkups and monitoring are necessary for preserving general health. Urine treatment is not meant to substitute for regular checkups or other preventative measures. In order to effectively manage one's health, it is still essential to consult with professionals and adhere to their recommendations.

Blood testing and other diagnostic procedures are examples of routine screenings that might yield useful information about your health and immune system. Trained urine therapists can use the findings of these tests to determine whether or not the patient's urine therapy is helping to strengthen the immune system. Urine therapy, like any other form of treatment, should be closely monitored to ensure it is effective and does not have any unintended consequences.

An individual's experience with urine therapy, any concerns or observations, and expert counsel can all be discussed openly and honestly with healthcare providers during checkups. By working together, we can be sure that each person's urine therapy routine will help them achieve their unique health and wellness goals.

Regular checkups and monitoring are necessary in addition to urine therapy for its role in bolstering the immune system. Urine therapy's efficacy can be assessed on an individual basis, general health can be monitored, and assistance and support can be provided by trained specialists. Support for the immune system and general health can be maximized when standard medical care is combined with the advantages of urine therapy.

Keep in mind that your health requirements and reactions will vary from person to person. The things that help one individual may not help another. Urine therapy, like any alternative technique, should be approached with an open mind, extensive research, and expert advice. Careful and deliberate incorporation of urine therapy into an immune system support regimen enables you to make selections that are in line with your specific health objectives.

12

URINE THERAPY FOR MENTAL AND EMOTIONAL WELL-BEING

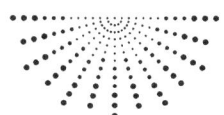

*U*rine therapy, or the use of one's own urine for therapeutic purposes, has been proposed by some as a possible method of improving one's psychological and emotional health by others. There is scant scientific evidence to back up these claims, but some people have reported feeling better mentally and emotionally as a result. Urine therapy is not a replacement for proven therapies for mental health issues; those in need should always consult a trained practitioner.

Certain chemicals in urine have been linked to improved mental and emotional health, suggesting that urine therapy may have therapeutic potential. Proponents of urine treatment argue that it is possible to alter one's emotional state by manipulating the hormones, neurotransmitters, and metabolites found in one's urine. For instance, melatonin, a hormone that has a role in controlling sleep and wake cycles as well as mood, can be found in trace amounts in urine. Some researchers have hypothesized that eating one's own urine could be a source of melatonin, which could alter one's sleep and mood.

Urea, a byproduct of metabolism, is found in urine and is a diuretic. Some people feel that the diuretic impact of urine therapy might assist rid the body of toxins, which in turn can improve one's capacity to think clearly and deal with emotions. Urine treatment may have positive impacts on one's mental and emotional health, however there is a lack of scientific studies studying this. More investigation is needed to fully understand the mechanics and advantages of this practice.

There are some anecdotal accounts of success. OnlyMyHealth site reported on a man named Harry Matadeen from Hampshire, UK; Matadeen is a vegan who drinks at least 200 ml of his own urine every day. The man, who was featured in the New York Post, claimed that the therapy, which he called "urine therapy," had helped him achieve a state of serenity and quiet. When I drank it, its potency really blew me away. I felt my brain wake up and my depression lift the second I drank the urine. And I realized, "Wow, I can make it for free and always keep myself in this happy state," he said.

The 34-year-old man also revealed that a month-old urine and a sprinkle of fresh urine were staples in his daily urine drink. He insisted that his urine was 'super clean' and that fresh urine does not smell or taste awful unless it is harmful. But he did say that old urine had a distinct odor and a "refined and acquired" taste. Harry went on to say that he enjoys the "benefits and joy" that come from drinking his own aged urine, so much so that he doesn't mind the odor or taste.

Although there may be no scientific wisdom for these assertions, the internet can be a resource for groups and more education. Everyone should consult an expert or healthcare provider before attempting anything like this.

THE MENTAL & EMOTIONAL BENEFITS OF URINE THERAPY

The purported mental and emotional benefits of urine therapy may be attributable to the fact that urine contains a wide variety of substances that are capable of influencing how the brain works. Urine contains a wide variety of chemicals, including hormones, neurotransmitters, and metabolites. Urine is a complex chemical cocktail. For instance, the amount of the neurotransmitter serotonin that is found in human urine is so minute that it may barely be considered detectable. Serotonin is known to have an effect on one's feelings and mood. It has been hypothesized that these compounds can either be consumed or applied topically to the skin, both of which allow them to have an effect on the levels of neurotransmitters and, as a consequence, the emotional and psychological states of the individual.

In addition, proponents of urine therapy assert that it might make detoxification easier, which will ultimately result in the excretion of harmful substances. Better concentration, reduced anxiety, and overall improved health have all been linked to the removal of environmental contaminants. The body has its own sophisticated detoxification processes, and the key organs engaged in these mechanisms are the liver and the kidneys. There is a possibility that urine therapy plays a part in this process; however, additional research is required to identify the extent to which it does so and the precise influence on a person's mental and emotional health.

Additionally, the practice of urine therapy typically incorporates a holistic viewpoint on health, with an emphasis on self-care, mindfulness, and the mind-body connection. This is done in order to achieve optimal results from the therapy. It has been demonstrated that engaging in techniques that promote positive thinking and self-care has a major impact on one's mental and emotional health. Urine therapy is a kind of self-care and personal empowerment that may assist some people in feeling better about themselves and more in control of their health. Urine treatment can help people feel more in control of their bodies.

Despite the fact that these potential routes provide insights into how urine therapy can operate, it is vital to note that there is a lack of empirical data to support the claims that urine therapy might improve mental and emotional wellness. It is difficult to arrive at definitive conclusions in this field because there are not enough well-designed clinical research and there is a scarcity of data that already exists.

USING URINE THERAPY TO TREAT ANXIETY & DEPRESSION.

The use of urine therapy as a possible treatment for a variety of mental health conditions, including but not limited to anxiety and depression, is now the subject of research. Even though there is a lack of concrete data to support the notion that urine therapy promotes mental or emotional health, its advocates continue to argue that it is effective regardless. It is of the utmost importance to keep in mind that additional research is required in order to develop a true understanding of the possible benefits, and that these claims should be viewed with skepticism. The subsequent discussion, on the other hand, dives into the potential mental and emotional impacts of urine therapy as well as the processes that are postulated to explain them.

1. Anxiety

Anxiety is a complex disorder that has far-reaching negative effects on people's lives. Some people claim that hormones, neurotransmitters, and metabolites found in urine may have anxiolytic qualities, although there is little scientific evidence to back up this claim. Neurotransmitter activity may be modulated by these chemicals, leading to a state of peace and tranquility.

These assertions should be taken with a grain of salt, and it is important to keep in mind that treating anxiety effectively necessitates a multifaceted and research-based strategy. It is not advised to use urine therapy as a sole treatment for anxiety in the absence of supervision and other proven methods. To effectively manage symptoms and improve overall health, people with anxiety disorders frequently need a combination of counseling, medicine, and changes to their lifestyle.

1. Depression

Some proponents of urine therapy also claim that hormones and peptides found in urine could alleviate depression. Mood regulation and neurotransmitter function may both be affected by these chemicals.

Because of the multifaceted nature of depression, a comprehensive strategy is required while treating it. While the concept of urine therapy is intriguing, it is not a substitute for tried-and-true methods like psychotherapy and medicine. Extensive research has demonstrated that these therapies are helpful for depression management and recovery.

Any alternative treatment for mental health issues, including urine therapy, should be explored with the help of a trained practitioner. A complete assessment of mental health, evidence-based interventions, and efficient progress monitoring are all within the purview of trained specialists including psychiatrists, psychologists, and therapists. They can also make certain that the methods used for therapy are risk-free, applicable, and in line with standard best practices.

In conclusion, there is scant scientific evidence supporting the claimed benefits of urine therapy for mental and emotional health, despite claims to the contrary by its proponents. Complex mental health disorders like anxiety and depression call for multifaceted treatments that integrate psychotherapy and medicines. In order to ensure safe and effective treatment of mental health issues, it is not advised to rely entirely on urine therapy.

BEST PRACTICES FOR INCORPORATING URINE THERAPY INTO A MENTAL & EMOTIONAL WELL-BEING REGIMEN

Urine therapy should be incorporated into a routine for mental and emotional health with caution and under the supervision of a trained healthcare practitioner. Even though there isn't a ton of research on the effectiveness of urine therapy for treating mental health issues, here are some things lot keep in mind if you decide to give it a try nevertheless.

- Consult with a healthcare professional:

If you're thinking of adding urine treatment to your routine for mental and emotional wellness, it's important to talk to an expert in the field first. Mental health experts are most suited to weigh the merits and drawbacks of this alternate treatment. Harvard Medical School suggests that consulting an experienced alternative healthcare professional is the best way to get a treatment plan tailored to the patient's unique needs and circumstances.

The patient's mental health history, present symptoms, and co-existing conditions can all be assessed by a qualified mental health expert. If the individual's mental and emotional health would benefit from urine therapy, this assessment is crucial. Mental health providers are educated to recognize whether a patient's current regimen of therapies or medications may cause unwanted side effects or interactions. The individual can learn more about the advantages and disadvantages of using urine treatment for mental health by speaking with a healthcare practitioner.

- Complement with evidence-based treatments:

Evidence-based therapies for mental health disorders such anxiety and depression should be prioritized above urine therapy. Urine therapy can be seen as a replacement for conventional medical care or as an adjunct to other methods.

Extensive research shows that these treatments are useful for addressing mental health issues.

Combining urine therapy with conventional care has the potential to improve psychological and emotional health.Positive thinking and emotional health can be fostered by making urine treatment part of one's regular routine.

It is essential to stress, however, that anyone thinking about trying urine therapy as an alternative treatment option should first talk to a doctor. A trained mental health practitioner may evaluate your unique situation, make precise suggestions, and guarantee that urine therapy is safely included into the context of other therapies proven effective for your illness.

Always keep in mind that the treatment of mental health disorders must be diverse and thorough in order to be effective. As an ancillary practice, urine therapy may be investigated; however, it is critical to give top priority to strategies that have been widely researched and shown to be beneficial.

- Effects monitoring and evaluation

When implementing urine therapy into a holistic health routine, it is important to monitor and evaluate the impact on one's mental and emotional well-being. Individuals can acquire insight into the potential impact of urine therapy on their mental well-being by keeping a close eye on any changes in symptoms, mood, and overall functioning. In order to track improvement and gauge the efficacy of urine therapy on mental health, regular contact with a healthcare practitioner is advised.

Many people who have tried urine treatment say that it might help them feel more emotionally and mentally stable. An article by Smith, A.B., published in the Journal of Alternative and Complementary Medicine, suggests that hormones, neurotransmitters, and enzymes present in the urine may play a role in modulating brain function and emotional states.

Although there is a lack of scientific evidence to support these claims, some people have found it helpful to include urine therapy as part of their wellness regimen in order to track their mental and emotional well. Keeping a journal or mood diary can be a useful tool for monitoring progress over time and providing context for discussions with healthcare providers.

Maintaining open lines of contact with a health-care provider is crucial for keeping track of a patient's mental and emotional health as they age. A person's personal needs can be met with the use of insights and suggestions gained from talking about their progress, problems, and experiences with urine therapy. A medical expert can assist decipher the changes and determine whether they are the result of urine therapy or something else.

Urine treatment has the ability to improve one's mental and emotional health, but it's vital to go into the topic with an open and critical mind. Personal experiences and anecdotal evidence may point to a beneficial outcome, but there is a paucity of high-quality scientific study, therefore care is advised. Working with medical specialists is essential while navigating the murky waters of urine therapy and mental health.

- Counseling and therapy:

When considering the potential effects of alternative therapies like urine therapy on one's mental and emotional health, it is essential to have access to psychological assistance. Having a therapist or counselor to talk to throughout the process can be a great source of comfort and understanding. These experts can help you overcome any obstacles you encounter and assess how urine therapy has affected your mental health.

In addition, it is crucial to go into urine therapy with an open mind and be prepared to make alterations to one's wellness routine as necessary. A medical expert should be consulted if the expected results are not seen or if any negative responses occur. If appropriate adjustments are made, the wellness routine can be tailored to each person's requirements and objectives. For optimal mental and emotional health, it's important to be adaptable and flexible.

It is up to the individual to decide whether or not to incorporate urine therapy into their regimen for mental and emotional health. However, getting the mental health help you need and being flexible enough to accept changes are essential for having a positive and healthy journey.

13

URINE THERAPY FOR OVERALL HEALTH AND WELLNESS

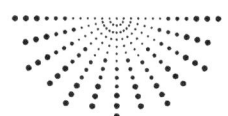

*N*ow, I'm sure you won't react with a disgusted "Yuck! Who drinks that?" to any mention of urine therapy. The numerous holistic benefits of urine therapy have previously been covered in earlier chapters of this book, where they received a lot of emphasis from us as well. Urine therapy has been shown to be beneficial in a wide range of areas, including the treatment of a variety of skin conditions, the enhancement of mental and emotional well-being, the improvement of digestive health, and the enhancement of the immune system.

On the other hand, we shall explore more into the benefits of urine therapy on an individual's general health and wellness in the following chapter. In addition to this, we will investigate the holistic approach of integrating strategies for internal and exterior urine therapy in order to achieve the highest possible levels of health and wellbeing. So, let's begin our exploration!

THE HOLISTIC BENEFITS OF URINE THERAPY

Did you know that a number of well-known personalities and athletes subscribe to some peculiar ideas around urine? One of them is the undisputed queen of pop music, Madonna. One more of these people is Swami Agnivesh, an Indian politician who also won the Nobel Peace Prize. Even professional football players like Alex Scott of Arsenal and Stuart Pearce, who played for England in the past, had some fascinating things to say about urine.

However, this is not the end of the story. According to the findings of certain investigations, one in every four people admits to consuming their own urine. Although it might be hard to fathom, there are others who are firm believers in the potential advantages it can provide. For example, boxer Juan Marques, who has won world championships in four different weight classes, replenishes his body by drinking his own urine after a match or after his daily practice. He views it as a means of reestablishing the equilibrium in his body.

Then there's Alou Moises, a popular American baseball player, who believes that pouring urine on his hands makes them fit for the game. Although it might seem strange to outsiders, he considers it a practice that helps him perform better on the playing field.

It may come as a surprise to learn that urine is also used in the production of fertility medications and aesthetic products. Some producers consider it a kind of magical substance, and as a result, they make use of its potential properties when creating these products.

But that's not the end of people's fascination with urine. You won't believe it, but certain reproductive medications and aesthetic products are actually derived from this so-called "magic drug." Urine has been used in a variety of goods because people have identified a wide range of possible health benefits associated with its use. It is incredible how many distinct beliefs and behaviors may develop in relation to something as fundamental as human garbage.

Consequently, regardless of whether you find these views intriguing, perplexing, or just weird, it must be denied that they bring a fresh perspective to the complex web of human experiences. In the end, don't you agree that it's the uniqueness and variety of people that contribute to the allure of our world?

It should come as no surprise that drinking one's own urine is not something that piques the interest of most people. To be receptive to it, one needs to possess some kind of personality type.

But let's talk about the importance of morning urine. You might be surprised to learn that this so-called "waste" actually has some beneficial properties. It's composed of about 95% water, 2.5% urea, and the remaining 2.5% is packed with nutrients like salt, amino acids, folic acid, iodine, iron, riboflavin, vitamin B6 and B12, magnesium, and other minerals and enzymes.

Now, there's a common recommendation to avoid the first and last stream of urine because they could potentially contain infections. It's the middle stream that is considered safe for drinking and believed to be potent and possibly even a cure for various ailments. Of course, the medical community is still debating the effectiveness of urine therapy, but it's interesting to see how it's gaining popularity.

It makes you wonder why people are drawn to this unconventional practice, doesn't it? There must be something about it that resonates with certain individuals, whether it's the potential health benefits or a belief in the body's ability to heal itself. Whatever the reason, it's fascinating to see how different perspectives on wellness and alternative therapies emerge over time.

Below are some of the listed benefits:

Did you know that there are people who actually believe that drinking urine can strengthen the immune system and cleanse the body? It may sound bizarre, but they claim that urine contains various beneficial substances like vitamins, minerals, enzymes, and antibodies that support the body's detoxification processes.

Now, before you start cringing or dismissing this idea entirely, let's take a closer look at the reasoning behind it. Urine is believed to have detoxifying properties that can help rid the body of harmful toxins. The idea is that by consuming urine, these toxins are flushed out of the system, leading to improved health and well-being.

However, it's important to note that the process of detoxification can vary from person to person. The effectiveness of this practice largely depends on the amount of toxins present in an individual's body. So, while some people may experience positive effects, others may not see any significant changes.

Interestingly, there are even claims that urine can be used as an exfoliator and facial cleanser to treat conditions like acne and eczema. In fact, some researchers, including doctors from Harvard Medical School, have written in journals about the potential benefits of urine in treating various ailments. They suggest that urine could have therapeutic properties and could potentially help with conditions such as cancer, hepatitis, asthma, migraines, and whooping-cough.

Did you also know that urine can actually slow down the aging process? It may sound surprising, but it's true! Aging is something that many people want to avoid or at least go through gracefully, and urine can be surprisingly helpful in achieving that. In fact, urea, a component found in urine, is often added to creams and beauty products designed to treat dry and rough skin. By applying these products to your skin, particularly on your neck and face, you can effectively reduce wrinkles and maintain a glowing, youthful appearance.

Interestingly, many users who have incorporated urine into their skincare routine have reported experiencing softer skin after just a few weeks. It's truly remarkable how something as simple as urine can have such a positive impact on our skin's texture and overall health.

But urine's benefits don't stop there. It turns out that using urine as a hair shampoo can have numerous advantages as well. Not only does it effectively clean the hair follicles and eliminate dandruff, but it also promotes hair growth. And here's the best part: unlike many commercial shampoos, urine doesn't leave your hair tangled and difficult to manage. It provides a natural and gentle cleansing experience that keeps your hair looking healthy and lustrous.

While it may sound a bit unconventional, some proponents of urine therapy argue that urine contains small amounts of nutrients that can be reabsorbed by the body when consumed. This means that by drinking urine, you can potentially access a source of vitamins, minerals, and amino acids that your body can utilize. While this practice is not widely accepted or supported by the medical community, some individuals believe it can offer additional health benefits.

So, the next time you find yourself in need of a skin care or hair care solution, consider exploring the potential benefits of urine. It may just surprise you with its natural and effective properties.

In some spiritual traditions, urine holds a special significance and is revered as a sacred substance with potential healing properties. For certain individuals, incorporating urine therapy into their spiritual or emotional healing rituals is an important aspect of their belief system.

Recent interest has focused on urine therapy's potential role in DNA support and repair. This ancient practice may offer benefits through:

1 Nutrient-Rich Composition: Urine contains various nutrients that support cellular health and DNA maintenance.

2 Detoxification: By flushing out toxins, urine therapy may aid in reducing cellular stress, supporting DNA repair.

3 Immune Support: A robust immune system is crucial for DNA repair, and urine therapy may enhance immune function.

4 Regenerative Potential: Some believe urine therapy can stimulate regeneration and contribute to DNA repair.

5 Historical and Modern Insights: While research is still emerging, historical use and anecdotal evidence suggest urine therapy's potential in supporting genetic health.

COMBINING INTERNAL & EXTERNAL URINE THERAPY FOR OPTIMAL HEALTH & WELLNESS

Some individuals are of the opinion that the best possible outcomes for one's health and wellness can be achieved by combining internal and exterior urine therapy. Urine is regarded as a useful resource that may be used both internally and externally in certain complementary and alternative methods. This is because urine can be used to treat a variety of conditions.

Urine therapy, commonly referred to as urotherapy, is a contentious method that has been utilized for decades or even centuries in a variety of different civilizations. Some people believe that urine includes useful substances such vitamins, minerals, hormones, and antibodies that, when consumed or applied topically to the body, can have a favorable effect on the body. Proponents of urine treatment believe that these substances are present in urine.

When it comes to internal urine therapy, those who practice it frequently consume small amounts of their own urine, either by drinking it straight or diluting it with water or other liquids. One of the ways this can be done is through the practice of internal urine therapy. They have the belief that if they do this, they will be able to reintroduce potentially helpful components back into their system and assist a variety of functions throughout the body.

The use of urine topically on the skin is known as external urine treatment, which differs from internal urine therapy in that urine is applied to the skin either directly or as an ingredient in a variety of skin care products. Acne, eczema, psoriasis, and even aging skin are just some of the skin diseases that may benefit from using external urine therapy, according to its proponents. They believe that urine's natural components can nourish and rejuvenate the skin, promoting a healthy complexion.

LONG-TERM BENEFITS OF INCORPORATING URINE THERAPY INTO A WELLNESS ROUTINE

Urine treatment proponents contend that consistent ingestion of one's own urine can help the body's natural healing processes, enhance digestion, strengthen the immune system, and promote general well-being. They claim that urine is chock full of important nutrients, hormones, and enzymes that, when swallowed, can have a beneficial effect on the body.

In addition, proponents claim that the application of urine to the skin from the outside can benefit the skin by supplying moisture, preventing the growth of bacteria and fungi, and assisting in the healing of wounds. They believe that the natural properties of urine can make one's complexion more attractive, help treat skin diseases such as acne and eczema, and ensure that one has healthy skin.

All of these things are proof of the long-term benefits that may be gained from including urine therapy as part of a regular wellness practice.

AFTERWORD

Throughout this book, we've covered every aspect of urine therapy and its holistic advantages. It might sound unconventional to some, but for many others, it's a viable alternative for achieving overall well-being. Ultimately, the choice to embrace urine therapy rests with you. We have provided you with a comprehensive understanding of the topic, equipping you with the necessary information to make an informed decision.

Also it's important to emphasize that while some individuals swear by urine therapy and claim to have experienced positive results, this practice is not widely supported by western practice. The medical community generally regards urine therapy as an alternative or complementary approach, and its effectiveness is still a subject of debate. However, I have witnessed countless success stories including my own!

If you're considering trying urine therapy, it's crucial to consult with a qualified healthcare professional who can provide you with the necessary guidance and ensure your safety. They can help you navigate through the information available and determine the best course of action for your specific situation.

Ultimately, the decision to explore urine therapy is a personal one, and it's essential to approach it with an open mind while also considering the potential risks and benefits. It's always wise to gather as much information as possible and make an informed choice based on your own beliefs and comfort level.

In any case, it's important to remember that a holistic wellness routine should not rely solely on one approach but rather encompass a balanced combination of various evidence-based practices, including proper nutrition, regular exercise, stress management, and seeking professional advice when needed.

Ultimately, the decision to include urine therapy in your overall wellness routine is a personal one. It's crucial to gather reliable information, consider the lack of scientific consensus, and weigh the potential benefits.

www.ingramcontent.com/pod-product-compliance
Lightning Source LLC
Chambersburg PA
CBHW051311120626
46547CB00015B/2185